66°E

34°N

DAIKUNDI

NILI

URUZGAN

TARINKOT

MUSA QALA

GUMBAD

PASHMUL

QALAT

ZABUL

32°N

SIAH CHOY

ARGHANDAB RIVER

TO KABUL

MIZAN

ZHARI

KANDAHAR

SPERWAN GHAR

BAZAR-E-PANJWAYI

M'SUM GHAR

PANJWAYI

SPIN BOLDAK

KANDAHAR

REGISTAN
(RED) DESERT

REGIONAL COMMAND SOUTH

TURKMENISTAN

UZBEKISTAN

TAJIKISTAN

CHINA

AFGHANISTAN

INDIA

IRAN

REGIONAL
COMMAND
SOUTH

PAKISTAN

N
W   E
S

On the cover

The image on our front cover holds deep meaning for all members of the Posse. Ours was as tight a group as any serving in Afghanistan. We depended upon each other. This shot was taken by Greg "Mooner" Moon on April 21, 2006, at the end of our visit to the small village of Gumbad in Kandahar Province. There we met with tribal elders, soldiers of 7 Platoon from the 1st Battalion, Princess Patricia's Canadian Light Infantry, and members of our civilian military cooperation (CIMIC) team. By day's end we were thoroughly impressed with their success in re-establishing the presence of the Government of Afghanistan in the north of the province. The photo shows a Blackhawk lifting off to take me and some of the Posse back to Kandahar Airfield and our brigade headquarters. The four soldiers in silhouette are (left to right) Randy Payne, Rick Tucker, Dave Houthuyzen and Matt Dinning. They and the rest of the Posse returned by road. Tragically, the day after this photo was taken, their vehicles were hit by an IED, killing Matt, Randy, Bill Turner and Myles Mansell.

OPERATION
MEDUSA

OPERATION

THE FURIOUS BATTLE

THAT SAVED AFGHANISTAN

FROM THE TALIBAN

MEDUSA

MAJOR GENERAL (RET'D) **DAVID FRASER**
AND **BRIAN HANINGTON**

McCLELLAND & STEWART

Published simultaneously in the United States of America by McClelland & Stewart, a division of Penguin Random House Canada Limited, a Penguin Random House Company.

LIBRARY AND ARCHIVES CANADA CATALOGUING IN PUBLICATION

Fraser, David (Major-General), author
    Operation Medusa / Major General David Fraser, Brian Hanington.

Issued in print and electronic formats.
ISBN 978-0-7710-3930-0 (hardcover).—ISBN 978-0-7710-3931-7 (EPUB)

    1. Operation Medusa, 2006. 2. Afghan War, 2001- —Campaigns—Afghanistan— Panjwāi (District). 3. International Security Assistance Force (Afghanistan). 4. North Atlantic Treaty Organization—Armed Forces—Afghanistan. I. Hanington, Brian, author II. Title.

DS371.4123.O655F73 2018   958.104'7   C2017-904792-2
                                                    C2017-904793-0

Library of Congress Control Number is available upon request

Typeset in Electra by M&S, Toronto
Printed and bound in the USA

Endpaper maps © Stiff (Ottawa)

McClelland & Stewart,
a division of Penguin Random House Canada Limited,
a Penguin Random House Company
www.penguinrandomhouse.ca

1 2 3 4 5   22 21 20 19 18

Penguin
Random House
McCLELLAND & STEWART

To the families of all those who serve.
Our fight for justice in the ragged corners of the world
is possible only because you sacrifice so much yourselves.

CONTENTS

A NOTE ON THE LANGUAGE

When military authors write about military events, they often use terms and abbreviations specific to their occupation. The texts they publish will then appeal to experienced military readers as familiar and therefore legitimate. Using such terminology carries two risks, however. First, the military terms of one nation are not always those of another, even among those operating in English. Working with our coalition counterparts in Afghanistan, Canadian soldiers were often compelled to convert Canadian terms to those better understood by our American, British, Danish, Dutch and Romanian partners, and we had to work hard to make sure we understood their own terms correctly. Second, when civilian readers encounter military jargon, they may understand generally what's going on yet not appreciate the specifics hidden within the terminology. To manage both risks, we either explain each esoteric term when first encountered or avoid that term altogether. We hope our simple language will not lead any sharp-end readers to doubt the authenticity of our account. We do favour acronyms here and there to keep the overall heft of the book reasonable, but always show the full term nearby.

Spelling is another issue. Afghan words for places, people and things spring from local languages such as Pashto, Dari, Hazaragi, Uzbek, Turkmen, Balochi and Pashayi. Attempts through history to transliterate these terms into English have resulted in a wide variety of spellings with few conventions. For clarity we wish to be consistent.

Panjwayi, where much of the action takes place, is written elsewhere as Panjwaii, Panjwaye, Panjwai and Panjway. The district on the north bank of the Arghandab River that runs east to west through Kandahar Province is variously called Zheley, Zharey, Zharay, Zheri and Zheray. We write it as Zhari. The village of Pashmul may appear in other sources as Pashmol, Pāshmāl and Pazmul. Where possible confusion remains, we have made a note in the text. Lastly, the names of companies in Task Force 3-06 are written as A Company, Bravo Company and Charles Company, as those were the conventions used in theatre.

WHO'S WHO

A guide to the personalities we refer to in the text, with ranks held at the time*

CA **Abthorpe, Major Geoff,** officer commanding, Bravo Company 1 RCR

US **Bolduc, Lieutenant Colonel Don,** commanding officer, 1st Battalion, 3rd Special Forces Group

CA **Buchanan, Major David,** executive assistant

CA **Conrad, Lieutenant Colonel John,** commanding officer of 1 Service Battalion and the National Support Element (Feb 2006 to Aug 2006)

CA **Demiray, Padre Suleyman,** chaplain

CA **Dinning, Corporal Matt,** close protection team member

US **Eikenberry, Lieutenant General Karl,** commander, Operation Enduring Freedom

CA **Fraser, Brigadier General David,** commander, Regional Command South

US **Freakley, Major General Benjamin,** deputy commander operations, ISAF and commander, 10th Mountain Division

CA **Gasparotto, Major Mark,** officer commanding, 23 Field Squadron

CA **Gauthier, Lieutenant General Michel,** commander, Canadian Expeditionary Force Command

CA **Goodyear, Major Rick,** National Command Element comptroller

CA **Green, Christina,** development advisor, Regional Command South

CA **Harper, Right Honourable Stephen,** Prime Minister of Canada (Feb 2006–Nov 2015)

CA **Hawes, Corporal Jeff,** gunner in LAV turret

CA **Hetherington, Lieutenant Colonel Simon,** commanding officer, Kandahar provincial reconstruction team

CA **Hillier, General Rick,** chief of the defence staff, for Canada

CA **Hope, Lieutenant Colonel Ian,** commanding officer, Task Force Orion

CA **Houthuyzen, Corporal Dave,** close protection team member

CA **Irving, Sergeant William,** TAC commander

CA **Irwin, Lieutenant Colonel Robert (Brian),** chief of staff, Canadian National Support Element (after Aug 1, 2006)

CA **Isfeld, Pamela,** policy advisor, Regional Command South

US **Jones, General James Logan,** Supreme Allied Commander Atlantic

CA **Lavoie, Lieutenant Colonel Omer,** commanding officer, Task Force 3-06

CA **Leslie, Lieutenant General Andrew,** chief of the land staff, for Canada

CA **Lewis, Colonel Fred,** deputy commander, Canadian National Support Element (after Aug 1, 2006)

CA **Lussier, Major Andy,** officer commanding, ISTAR squadron

CA **MacKay, Peter,** Canada's minister of national defence (Aug 2007–Jul 2013)

CA **Martin, Right Honourable Paul,** Prime Minister of Canada (Dec 2003–Feb 2006)

CA **MacDonald, Chief Warrant Officer Michael,** brigade sergeant major, Regional Command South

CA **Moon, Master Corporal Gregory,** driver

CA **Muldoon, Corporal Al,** close protection team member

US **Nicholson, Colonel John,** commander, Regional Command East

CA **O'Connor, Right Honourable Gordon,** Canada's minister of national defence (Feb 2006–Aug 2007)

CA **Offrey, Corporal Jamie,** close protection team member

CA **Payne, Corporal Randy,** close protection team member

CA **Putt, Colonel Tom,** deputy commander, Canadian National Support Element (March–July, 2006)

UK **Richards, General Sir David,** commander, International Security Assistance Force

CA **Sajjan, Major Harjit,** liaison officer to the Governor of Kandahar

CA **Schreiber, Lieutenant Colonel Shane,** assistant chief of staff operations

CA **Sprague, Major Matthew,** officer commanding, Charles Company 1 RCR

US **Terry, Brigadier James,** deputy commander general operations, Combined Joint Task Force 76

CA **Tucker, Master Seaman Rick,** close protection team member

NL **Van den Bos, Colonel Willem,** deputy commander, Regional Command South

UK **Vernon, Colonel Christopher,** brigade chief of staff

CA **Walsh, Master Warrant Officer Shawn,** close protection team leader

US **Williams, Colonel Steve,** commander, Task Force Grizzly and deputy commander, Regional Command South

CA **Wright, Major Michael,** officer commanding, A Company 2 PPCLI, assigned to Task Force 3-06

* **CA** Canada

NL The Netherlands

UK United Kingdom

US United States

THE BATTLE THAT COULD NOT BE LOST

BY GENERAL THE LORD RICHARDS OF HERSTMONCEUX GCB CBE DSO

I assumed command of NATO forces in Afghanistan in early May 2006. At that time NATO was responsible only for the relatively benign regions of Kabul, and the north and west of the country. The real challenge for us all was still to come.

It had been agreed at NATO's Istanbul Summit in June 2004 that the NATO Alliance and its allies would assume responsibility from the Americans for the whole country less than two years later. I and my Allied Rapid Reaction Corps headquarters, based normally in Germany, were given the job. This of course included the province of Kandahar, the spiritual home of the Taliban and its leader Mullah Omar. Success in Kandahar would be central to NATO's fortunes.

Canada volunteered to provide the first commander of the troops in Kandahar and indeed of the turbulent south as a whole. That officer was Brigadier General David Fraser. On General Fraser's shoulders would lie the reputation and perceived prowess of NATO and its allies—as well, of course, as that of his Canadian contingent. He and his troops lay on what German military doctrine would call the operation's *schwerpunkt*, or point of main effort. If either he or they failed sufficiently to subdue the Taliban and impress the Afghan people—who five years earlier had succeeded in ridding themselves of the Taliban's malign rule over the whole country— then NATO too would fail.

For many years the Canadian Armed Forces had focused their efforts on blue-beret UN operations. Their much-respected war-fighting ethos of the First and Second World Wars had been seriously eroded. A dynamic new Chief of the Defence Staff, General Rick Hillier, was much troubled by this and saw operations in Afghanistan as an opportunity to restore Canada's fighting prowess and military reputation. The genesis of this transformation was to be in Kandahar, although he could not have anticipated the challenge it would pose.

On July 31, 2006 I took over command of the southern region of Afghanistan from my U.S. counterpart, Lieutenant General Karl Eikenberry. By then I had already visited David Fraser a number of times. David had been in theatre as the commander of Task Force Aegis for five months, and with his well-thought-out plans and Karl's generous-hearted cooperation, the change-of-command process was quick and efficient. To begin with all seemed fine, but then reports started to reach me in Kabul of a large build-up of Taliban forces in the Panjwayi area southwest of Kandahar City. NATO and Afghan intelligence suggested this was part of a determined Taliban plan to force our under-strength and inexperienced NATO troops to try to dislodge them from their strong defensive position, defeating us in the process.

The option to ignore the Taliban in Panjwayi was unacceptable both politically and militarily, as they dominated a key piece of geography that included the main highway between Kandahar and Herat, the nation's second and third-largest cities. And psychologically their presence posed a dominant and destructive influence over not just the people of the province but, given it was Mullah Omar's home, all the way to Kabul and beyond.

The Taliban were right. NATO had to attack and defeat them. If not, within a month of our taking over responsibility for the tougher provinces from the U.S., the perception would be that the Alliance was not up to the challenge. Afghan and wider international confidence in us would collapse and the Taliban would score a major victory. We had no alternative but to attack their increasingly strong and well-prepared positions, both to free up vital movement on the highway and, more importantly, to regain psychological ascendancy over the Taliban and restore confidence in NATO at a vital time. The principal means I had to meet this crucial challenge was the Canadian contingent under David Fraser. On his shoulders and that of his troops would lie NATO's fortunes.

This book tells the story of the vital Battle of Medusa, the codename given to the operation to attack and defeat the Taliban position in Panjwayi. It describes the huge pressures on contemporary military commanders like Fraser—exerted by political leaders at home and military leaders in their chain of command—and a non-negotiable imperative to succeed on the battlefield, often with insufficient troops and the wrong equipment. The brutally honest description of the ups and downs experienced by Fraser and his troops in this book makes for fascinating reading in the great tradition of battlefield history.

At times it was a close-run thing. But at the end, Canadian officers and the NATO coalition soldiers they led had triumphed. Hundreds of Taliban fighters were dead, wounded or had fled to nearby Pakistan. Rick Hillier's aim had surely been met. The Canadian Army—under a brave, determined and skilled commander in David Fraser, and with the expert and largely unsung help of Afghan, American, British, Dutch, Danish and Romanian troops—had performed with a courage and ferocity that dealt the Taliban a crippling blow. Canadian soldiers who had entered the battle with little or no combat experience proved in just two weeks that they were first-class warriors. Some had been killed and many more wounded in close-quarter fighting that was on occasion as brutal as any have faced. Thanks to all these soldiers NATO's reputation was saved, the Taliban were forced to think again, and the Afghan people had their faith in a better future restored.

Canada should be proud of those who fought in the Battle of Medusa. I certainly am. It was with barely suppressed emotion that a few days after the battle I accepted David Fraser's invitation to visit the field hospital and meet the wounded. I was greeted by soldiers with humour wonderfully undiminished, and was honoured to issue each the wound stripe to mark Canada's recognition of the sacrifice each had made. In this gesture, David Fraser did me a huge privilege, one that I shall never forget. Indeed, to the day I die, I will remain hugely proud that I can say, "I commanded Canadian troops in Afghanistan."

Here is their story.

BOND

T his is a book about Operation Medusa, a military battle fought in the Panjwayi District of Kandahar Province in Afghanistan in the first half of September 2006. The combatants were the Taliban on one side and a coalition of forces from many NATO nations on the other. As the subtitle of this book emphasizes, the battle was furious. It was also uniquely complex. Operation Medusa was the first major combat action ever led by NATO and the largest battle fought by Canadian troops since the Korean War. It was carried out under the command of NATO's International Security Assistance Force (ISAF), which less than a month before had taken responsibility for the region in which all the action would take place. The Canadian battalion task force numbered some 800 men and women who would soon shoulder the burden of much of the fighting. They had arrived in the country to begin their rotation just days before the battle. Most of them had never seen combat before.

Direct control of NATO coalition forces in the area was my responsibility. As a brigadier general, I was the Commander of Regional Command (South) based in Kandahar, a position I had taken back in February of 2006. So when Operation Medusa began, I had been in place with my brigade headquarters and a previous rotation of Canadian soldiers for long enough to understand the enormity of the challenges we faced. I was concerned.

As Book One of this volume makes clear, the run-up to Operation Medusa began almost a year before the battle as we readied our Canadian soldiers, aviators, sailors and special-forces operators to deploy. Almost immediately, things began to go wrong. As the obstacles mounted, we learned enough to understand deeply that the outcome of a fight on this scale with the Taliban was uncertain. The competing priorities of governments, departments, regions, militaries, agencies and even other wars made every single day a high-speed chase along multiple tracks. Even in the retelling, the sheer number of factors that affected us can be hard to keep straight. I have included many lists and glossaries to help readers avoid confusion.

Book Two tells the tale of the battle itself. While only two weeks in duration, it called upon every resource we had, every ally we knew, every favour we could call in and every tactic we could deploy to apply constant pressure to the enemy without falling into the many traps set for us. The unfolding events of Book Two will be best understood once you have the context detailed in Book One, but if you get twitchy, go ahead and flip to the fighting.

For now, let me explain something.

A military is only as effective as the individual teams upon which it is built. As such, when Canada agreed to take over Regional Command South in Afghanistan on behalf of the NATO coalition as of July 2006, we knew that the International Security Assistance Force (ISAF) would be effective only if our forces could all gel into a comprehensive combined and joint team, where *combined* means a force of troops from more than one nation and *joint* means a force of personnel from more than one military service, such as army with navy and air force.

Months earlier, we had looked hard at our own team first. Canadians would form a joint task force and a brigade headquarters that would command coalition efforts in the whole region. Together they would be called Task Force Aegis. When we gathered for the first time to conduct training in Wainwright, Alberta in the fall of 2005, we were a fractured if well-intentioned band of soldiers from a number of disparate regiments and corps. Many of our brigade headquarters staff would be coming from other countries; some of those but not all joined us to train. We were not yet a team. That would come in time, and time was our enemy.

Task Force Aegis was to be built on the core of the 1 Canadian Mechanized Brigade Group (1 CMBG), of which I had just taken command. We all needed to figure out how to work together, and this started with my office and personal team—which began with me, my personal assistant Trevor Friesen, my executive assistant David Buchanan, and our formation sergeant major Mike MacDonald. Our quartet quickly established a routine and we were relieved to discover that we worked well together. Satisfied, we then began building our tactical team, commonly called a TAC. This was the larger group of soldiers we'd need at brigade headquarters to man our small convoy of vehicles, and the communications and protection party that would allow us to operate safely as a unit in the field. Our TAC would evolve several times before we reached Afghanistan.

The leader of that tactical team was Sergeant Bill Irving from Lord Strathcona's Horse (Royal Canadians). Bill was a character—openhearted, opinionated, humorous and frequently profane. An outstanding soldier, he would soon prove to be the soul of our team. During our workups in Wainwright, Alberta, Bill established himself as our protector, guide and inspiration. Adopting us as his personal charges, he treated all of us with a classic parental mix of high expectation, strict discipline and deep empathy. It was fitting that we gave him the nickname Mother.

To our growing family we added a close protection team of members of the Canadian Forces Military Police, which had recently taken over from Joint Task Force 2 the responsibility for protection of all but the most senior of Canada's leaders. Afghanistan was their first mission, and I was their first assignment. When Mike MacDonald and I met that team in Edmonton, we were impressed. They were professional, determined, fit and ready for hell.

In Wainwright our growing band formed into a tight, mission-focused entity that gradually became known to each of us as the Posse. We openly admitted our individual strengths and weaknesses in an earnest effort to figure out how we could function as a high-performing unit. We lived and operated in close quarters, and our bond strengthened with

Sergeant Bill Irving was known to us all as Mother. Tactical commander of our team, Bill led us whenever we went outside the wire, typically three to four days each week. When training in Canada before our tour, I had asked for a team to man my LAV command vehicle in theatre. I was given an outstanding one. Lord Strathcona's Horse (Royal Canadians), an armoured regiment in my brigade, formed the core and added a close protection team of military police. These and others made up what we all soon referred to as the Posse. We became a family and, while I may have been thought of as the patriarch, the centre of the family was Bill. Mother was professional, tough as nails with a heart of gold, foul-mouthed as they come and generous to a fault. In my career I have never had more faith in any soldier of any rank. We laughed together, cried together and shared an openness that lasts to this day. Mother was my gauge on how the troops felt, never shying away from telling me what was and was not working. He was the only one in the formation I allowed to lecture me (always with good reason) about why we could not do what I had asked. Often it was as simple as insisting I comply with safety requirements (helmet, glasses, gloves, etc.). From time to time he gave me the finger, which I took as a signal that I was putting myself or someone in peril. That said, I am intrigued that a man to whom I have entrusted my life and whom I respect to this day can sip tea out of a cup and saucer with the proper finger etiquette. We must have caught Mother in a moment of weakness.

Mike MacDonald, whose artillery background inspired us to call him "Bomber," was our formation (brigade) sergeant major. In our headquarters, his cabin stood next to mine. Bomber and I had a ritual; we started every day with PT, followed by a cup of coffee in his cabin over which we discussed our soldiers, their morale and the situations they faced. Bomber had his finger on the pulse, which I greatly appreciated given the insane tempo we all maintained and the hundreds of dispersed teams we managed. I could trust the Bomber to let me know what was and was not working. A consummate soldier of few words, he was highly regarded by all, and he was my trusted confidant. Now I have to state for the record that every morning when we chatted in his cabin, the Bomber put on a country and western CD to create a supposedly relaxing atmosphere. But he had only one CD to his name, and so we listened to the same handful of country tunes day after day, month after month. Halfway through the tour, he announced that he had procured a brand new CD. I was thrilled, but not for long. When he put it on, I could tell it was new all right, but only a new copy of the same old CD. Oh well, one can never discount the value of routine and consistency. To this day I think back on the Bomber's skill and his advice with admiration and gratitude.

every passing day. As we refined our roles and routines, we became familiar with one another and soon started using nicknames. Bill Irving, of course, was Mother. I was the Boss. Mike MacDonald was Bomber, a nod to his artillery background and master-gunner designation. Our driver Greg Moon was Mooner. Our signaller Keith Brown was Brownie, while our close protection team member Adam Seegmiller was Seegy, and so on. All apt if not ingenious monikers. As with fighter pilots, when we found a name that fit someone we assigned it as a handle, a shortcut acknowledging that he or she was part of our close-knit unit. In this way, our Posse was no different than any other tactical grouping operating in RC South. Those working together in small teams under the arduous conditions in Afghanistan felt part of a family whose members admired, trusted and cared for each other. Not surprising. After all, tribal affiliation is the mechanism by which our species has survived and prospered.

We formed the Posse twelve years ago, and to this day we refer to each other as we did during our mission. After depending on a group for your very life, that life can come to feel a little empty without those comrades by your side. We were united by the adventures and horrors we lived through. When we bump into each other now on the street, we will often slip away for a cup of coffee or pint of beer and a round or two of war stories, as all veterans do.

In the months leading up to Operation Medusa, our brigade headquarters team grew to include a wider group that would be soon working out of our building at Kandahar Airfield. Many of them appear in the pages that follow for good reason. They each proved they could function under duress, applying their expert knowledge to help me to make life-and-death decisions within impossible timelines. My assistant chief of operations Shane Schreiber, senior planner Steve Carr, and my branch heads of intelligence and operations all knew one truth—that the men and women in the units who reported to the brigade depended on us for critical guidance and support. Establishing tight communication between our brigade headquarters and the commanding officers of every unit that rotated through Regional Command South became our priority.

A particular challenge we faced on the tour was to establish that same depth of communication with new, often unfamiliar units that joined our brigade while we were already moving at speed in theatre. In many cases the compressed timelines and accelerated tempo would not allow us to develop the close relationships we wanted. But we made it work and, on balance, Regional Command South was as tight an operation as we could build given the circumstances.

Tragically, casualties are something every military has to face. In peacetime there are accidents, whereas in war there are both accidents and losses from engagements. At every level, all of us serving in Afghanistan did everything we could to mitigate the threat to our men and women, but we could never remove it. So going in we admitted the gravity of our situation and prepared to face the horrid truth.

Nothing, however, did really prepare us for the death of our own. After a visit to Gumbad in the northern part of Kandahar Province in April, our Posse suffered its first casualties. I had departed by air with some of them while the remainder were to return by road. Greg Moon's photograph on the cover of this book was taken at exactly that moment. On their trip back, in convoy, those travelling overland hit an IED. Lieutenant Bill Turner, Bombardier Myles Mansell, Corporal Randy Payne and Corporal Matt Dinning were all killed. Mother managed the unimaginable scene with incredible support from Charlie Company's 7 Platoon led by Lieutenant Kevin Shamoo. When the call went out that our TAC had been hit, Kevin's team immediately jumped into their vehicles and drove to the site of the explosion. Their own vehicle was disabled enroute, so they immediately dismounted and ran the last kilometre to the incident site in full kit. In spite of the oppressive heat, Kevin's men sped to the assistance of other soldiers in need. This was just one of too many incidents during our tour where unimaginable things happened and where men and women do whatever is needed to help others. That philosophy of standing beside and taking care of each other made all of us tighter and stronger.

The Posse learned very early the horrors of the mission. That April incident was a sobering indoctrination to our new reality and the tremendous responsibility each of us would shoulder. The violent loss of our friends plagues us still, the kind of memory that tormented veterans keep to themselves or share only with others who have experienced the horrors of war.

> When I came back from Afghanistan, I didn't have the same kind of brotherhood camaraderie, and that terrified me. We all have demons. We're not the same as when we went there. Is it post-traumatic stress? Not sure. But I do notice that I need adrenaline on a daily basis and I seek it out.
>
> ADAM "SEEGY" SEEGMILLER

We travelled as the Posse and carried out full mission planning everywhere we went. Our tactical commander, Mother, conducted the planning as directed by my executive assistant David "Buck" Buchanan. We used either ground or air transportation depending on time and security considerations. During Operation Medusa we used helos for the most part to optimize the time I spent in my headquarters and with my units in the field. While deployed, I took a security team comprising specially trained military police, along with my brigade sergeant major Mike MacDonald, my communicator Keith Brown and my personal assistant Greg Chan. We always went as a team so we were able to operate as such should a tactical event happen.

This event shaped us and gave us the necessary strength and resilience we would need for those times we had to rely on each other even when not all of us were together due to leave or tactical situations. Our four friends were gone and they had to be replaced—though they could never be truly replaced. The members of the Posse together sought out and chose soldiers to augment our team. With such noble boots to fill, the new additions faced a difficult task, but they were welcomed warmly and fully, and we were soon able to carry on with our mission.

Having experienced true esprit de corps among our own Posse, Bomber and I then sought out that kind of spirit within all the command teams and units we visited in the region. We looked for the tightness, sense of familiarity, respect and trust a team needs to be effective. Where there was candid dialogue between officers, NCOs (non-commissioned officers) and soldiers, the unit could be depended upon to work well together. Where there was tension and distance among the troops, we knew we would have to spend more time helping put them on a better path.

In my career I have been part of many such outstanding teams, but the Posse will forever be the one that saw the most, suffered the worst, and yet endured by caring for each other. The stories we wrote through our shared experience and the lifelong bonds we forged are the greatest gifts I took from our mission. With that in mind, I proudly present the members of our team.

THE POSSE

TACTICAL COMMAND POST

Brownie	Master Corporal Keith Brown, commander's signaller
Buck	Major David Buchanan, executive assistant
Jackie Chan	Lieutenant Greg Chan, personal assistant
Boss	Brigadier General David Fraser, commander, Regional Command South
	Captain Trevor Friesen, personal assistant
Jeb	Corporal Jeff Hawes, gunner

Mother	**Sergeant Bill Irving,** TAC commander
Bomber	**Chief Warrant Officer Mike MacDonald,** formation sergeant major
Mooner	**Corporal Gregory Moon,** driver
	Janan Mustafa, interpreter
	Corporal Aaron Pope, gunner
	Corporal John Hodges, gunner

CLOSE PROTECTION TEAM

Project Bryant	**Corporal Kane Bryant**
	Corporal Matt Dinning (KIA, April 2006)
	Corporal Dave Houthuyzen
	Bombardier Myles Mansell (KIA, April 2006)
Dooner	**Corporal Allan Muldoon**
	Corporal Jamie Offrey
	Corporal Randy Payne (KIA, April 2006)
Seegy	**Corporal Adam Seegmiller**
Bluto	**Master Seaman Rick Tucker,** close protection team second-in-command
	Lieutenant William Turner (KIA, April 2006)
	Master Warrant Officer Shawn Walsh, close protection team leader

BOOK ONE
THE RUN-UP

To better visualize the events leading to
Operation Medusa, refer to the run-up chart
inside the front cover.

CHAPTER 1

REACT

This mission was a brutal wake-up call for the CAF. Very much needed. We got so much street cred with our allies for punching above our weight, it's insane.

MOTHER

I t all started like this.

One day after the attacks of September 11, 2001, the United Nations Security Council condemned the aggression, offered its sympathy to Americans and clarified that members of the United Nations had a right to individual and collective self-defence. It urged the worldwide suppression of terrorism and asked that all who commit such acts and all those who aid or harbour them be held accountable.

Eight days after that, Canada's Minister of National Defence declared that Canadian Armed Forces personnel serving on military exchange programs abroad were welcome to participate in local operations responding to the attacks.

Eight days after that, the UN Security Council prescribed methods by which member states should root out terrorist organizations and deprive them of the funds and materials they needed to operate.

Six days after that, NATO's North Atlantic Council declared that any attack on a member nation would be interpreted as an attack on all NATO nations.

Three days after that, Prime Minister Jean Chrétien announced that Canada was sending aviators, soldiers and sailors to join the international anti-terrorist force known as Operation Enduring Freedom. Canadian efforts would themselves be codenamed Operation Apollo. Units of the Canadian Armed Forces were put on immediate notice.

The day after that, the defence minister deployed Canadian warships to the Gulf, and announced that some 2,000 Canadian Armed Forces personnel would be assigned to Operation Apollo.

And so it began.

CHAPTER 2

COMMIT

I'm not a cliché guy, but the burden of leadership is just that, a burden. You have to make decisions that will affect every man and woman under your command. Lives may be shattered, but you still have to have the balls to make those decisions and stand behind them.

MOTHER

It was Paul Martin's government that finally gave the green light for the Kandahar mission. Rick Hillier—our Chief of the Defence Staff at the time—warned that this was going to be a really tough mission. There would be casualties. Rick was a forceful communicator and used every rhetorical trick in the book to convince his betters to get on board. He also helped warm Canadians to the idea by talking to the media, famously characterizing the Taliban as "detestable murderers and scumbags" who "detest our freedoms . . . detest our society . . . detest our liberties." With such invocations he helped secure Canadian concurrence that the cause was just and that the pursuit of such a cause might be worth risking and losing Canadian lives.

So under the Martin government, the imminent thrust into Afghanistan was clearly articulated. Then the government changed. In November 2005, a motion of no confidence was passed by the House of Commons, and Stephen Harper's Conservatives then formed a minority government after a federal election in late January 2006.

The appointment of Gordon O'Connor as Minister of National Defence—a retired brigadier general with over thirty years' army experience—raised expectations of broad support for the military, at least within the ranks of the Canadian Armed Forces who saw him as one of our own. With Canada's forces ready to ship out, a second battalion in the wings, and a brigade group trained and ready to take over command of Regional Command South with full responsibility for military operations in Nimroz, Helmand, Kandahar, Zabul, Uruzgan and Daikundi provinces, the minister's experience gave us a considerable level of comfort. We could see that the Harper government was committed to the NATO coalition and the three-part role Canada was about to play. In time, the phrase *defence, development and diplomacy* was widely used in Canadian discussions and documents to acknowledge that force alone could not do the job that needed doing.

That job was to be in Kandahar. In some circles, it's still in vogue to presume that Canada ended up in Kandahar because it took us so long to commit and all the better spots were gone. Not true.

Lieutenant General Michel Gauthier was on hand as the choice was made. Mike was an engineer officer by training and would be the general named to command the Canadian Expeditionary Forces Command (CEFCOM). This was a new command that began during our rotation into Afghanistan. The planning for Afghanistan was done with two groups inside NDHQ; the outgoing Deputy Chief of the Defence Staff (DCDS Group) and the new CEFCOM. CEFCOM then would take over the duties of the DCDS and become the CDS' national commander for all domestic and international operations. From Afghanistan we reported to CEFCOM on Canadian national matters, much as we reported to OEF and later ISAF on regional matters. Mike was a details guy with an insatiable thirst for information. I had worked with him before and understood that if I could share everything we were reading, writing, recording and watching in theatre with him, he would take the time to digest it all and be better able to support us. He told me how the decision to be in Kandahar was made.

NATO assumed responsibility initially for the Kabul area of ops in summer 2003 and Canada stepped up right away, assuming lead responsibility for Kabul from 2003 to 2004. It was always intended to be just one year. I can't remember exact numbers but it was a brigade headquarters, an infantry battalion, plus other bits and pieces—probably just shy of 2,000 soldiers. Later in 2003, NATO expanded to Regional Command North, with the Germans taking the lead. Concurrently we signed up for the ISAF leadership role, with Rick Hillier acting as COMISAF [commander of the ISAF] from February to August 2004. He was therefore in a very good position to advise Canada on possible courses of action following our handover to others in Kabul. Next in order was Regional Command West, and nations were approached initially in the summer of 2004. I remember Canada being involved in the conversation in the early fall of 2004, and we actually sent a recce party to western Afghanistan at that time. But we were just wrapping up our major mission in Kabul and needed an operational pause. We weren't ready to sign up for another major mission. We were tapped out. Coincidentally, the Italians had already signed up for leadership of RC West by the time of our recce, and took the most visible and accessible locations. Our recce party reported back that two or three provincial reconstruction team (PRT) locations were available, yet all of these were in sparsely populated areas where our efforts could only have limited impact, especially given the considerable resupply and logistics challenges in these remote locations. In such a situation, our troops would have been exposed for very little potential effect. NATO pressed us to take one of them, but it made no sense to us. I participated as Chief of Defence Intelligence in a memorable video conference with SACEUR [Supreme Allied Commander Europe], our CDS [Chief of the Defence Staff] Ray Henault and others, where they pushed us very hard. But the Canadian military recommendation was not to sign up for any of the available PRT locations in RC West, even though they may have been "safer" than

Mike Gauthier, Fred Lewis and Gordon O'Connor.

Lieutenant General Mike Gauthier was my Canadian commander. An engineer, he was Rick Hillier's operational commander in the Canadian Expeditionary Force Command (CEFCOM) for all Canadian international operations, based in Ottawa. Mike and I talked daily, normally after my day was done and my meetings with either the 10th Mountain Division (under Operation Enduring Freedom) or NATO had concluded. We would recap the day's events and talk about what was to come next. Mike had a huge capacity for digesting information, but the reports he needed took us too long to prepare, had too many omissions and simply didn't give him the view from theatre he needed. We changed our reporting procedures and instead I sent him everything that I saw (in the raw), and added my assessment on top of that. While the staff in Ottawa were initially over-whelmed with the volume of information, we all became better able to sense what was going on half a world away from each other. Whenever something bad happened, I would call Mike, which was normally at night when he was asleep. I spoke more often than not to his wife, whom I had just awoken; eventually I advised Mike to move the telephone to his side of the bed. We worked well together. He always supported me in theatre, which was essential, as the relentless tempo of Medusa and our frequent need to adapt to keep the initiative as the Taliban acted meant that our plans had to be fluid. "Fight the enemy guided by a plan" was our motto. The key interlocutor between our in-theatre team and Ottawa was my national deputy, Colonel Fred Lewis. Fred rotated in with 1 RCR and immediately got up to speed. Another engineer, he was always good-natured, thoughtful and a joy to work with. He kept Ottawa informed on the details of what was happening day-to-day, hour-to-hour, minute-to-minute. He was one very busy deputy. The polit-ical authority on top of us all was Gordon O'Connor, our Minister of National Defence. A former military officer, he understood our world and what we needed. Some might say he was gruff, but he did more than anyone else to get us the materiel we needed. We'd brief him on the require-ments, he'd conduct his due diligence, and then we would find our requirements met. I have never been better supported in any mission as I was by my chain of command—especially from a materiel point of view. Ottawa, in its entirety, pulled together for the troops in the field. Not to say that we always agreed, but the speed at which we were responded to has to be credited in great part to Mike Gauthier and Gord O'Connor. And without a great deputy like Fred Lewis, I would have spent a lot more of my time looking back to Ottawa instead of onto the field of battle, which would have endangered the mission.

other areas. We wanted to be somewhere we could make a difference. That logic was accepted at the political level.

MIKE GAUTHIER

The UK was also keen to lead RC South, but owing to their major
troop commitment in Iraq they could not do so at the time NATO had
committed to. Growing insecurity in Iraq in 2004 and 2005 had shaped
the expansion timeline in Afghanistan. The U.S. was eager to shift
most American troops, equipment and combat air support from
Afghanistan to Iraq to bring that conflict to a conclusion. To that end
they asked that RC South be fully commanded by NATO by the summer
of 2006. And while the authorities in the UK were eager to get out of
Iraq, they could do so only at a certain pace; they would not be ready
to assume command of RC South until 2007. So Canada stepped up.

In November 2004, we began informal discussions with the British
and the Dutch about teaming up in Regional Command South.
We had worked with both nations to positive effect over a number
of years in one of the regions in Bosnia, and therefore were comfortable with the idea of replicating this partnership of like-minded
nations in southern Afghanistan. We understood fully that southern
Afghanistan would be substantially more difficult than the west in
terms of the strength of the Taliban, although we did not appreciate
how much stronger the insurgency would grow from 2005 to 2007
and beyond. As discussions progressed over a period of months, it
became clear that the UK could not immediately assume the lead
role in RC South in line with the NATO anticipated timeline of
summer 2006, and they urged us to take the first command rotation.

In late 2004 we began to look seriously at playing this leadership role and, along with it, basing our forces in Kandahar—which,
owing to the already well-established coalition base and airfield
there, we judged to be wise. Helmand and the other provinces
were too remote for our liking. Canada initially approved assuming

responsibility for the Kandahar PRT in early 2005, and several months later approved and announced that we would take on the initial RC South command role with the understanding that leadership would rotate among RC South partner nations. We would also provide a battalion for Kandahar Province (as well as the PRT), which the NATO ISAF request for forces had called for. The decision to go to Kandahar was initially a decision about committing to a PRT (under U.S. Operation Enduring Freedom) beginning in August of 2005. The subsequent and more difficult decision was to commit to the RC South leadership role as well as the battalion in Kandahar, and I believe this was announced by the government in August or September 2005, perhaps a bit later. The former was made with eyes wide open about the potential for the latter. All of these decisions and associated deliberations were made by the Martin government during its two-year tenure.

All of this was done very deliberately, in full consultation with NATO allies and the Americans (who had the pre-NATO coalition lead) over a period of many months and multiple recces. We most certainly were not backed into Kandahar. We believed we could handle it, very much predicated on provision of enablers and support by U.S. forces in place. We also welcomed the opportunity to play the leadership role in this difficult challenge and were confident we were up to it.

MIKE GAUTHIER

Before heading to Afghanistan in early 2006, I had to consider how many Canadians might be killed in theatre. Everyone likes to pretend there is no longer an acceptable body count in a military campaign, but that's more political imperative than practical habit. For generals, knowing the possible butcher's bill is essential. Before heading over to take command of RC South, I reviewed the details of every enemy engagement encountered by the Americans who had proceeded us. Combining data about such military metrics as contact type, location and force ratios,

I extrapolated from numbers of dead and wounded to arrive at an estimate of what we might experience. I showed it to Rick Hillier and the
guys on the Joint Strategic Assessment Committee using a PowerPoint
deck to explain the process I had used. Then I unveiled my expected
death toll. We would lose between forty and forty-two Canadians between
February and November of 2006. Hillier nodded and said, "Great. Now
take that slide out and never show it again." End of discussion. I learned
later that he never even raised the figure with General Michel Gauthier,
the head of the Canadian Expeditionary Force Command (CEFCOM) to
whom I would be reporting from theatre.

> I never heard any estimate of likely casualties. Not once. But I can
> tell you that as they began to tally up during the rotation, I noted
> the resilience of the political leadership in relation to the mission.
> There were deaths. Bodies came home. Yet even as repatriation
> ceremonies escalated, I never had an indication from the CDS or
> through him from the political realm that anyone had a problem
> with what we were doing in Afghanistan . . . until Medusa.
>
> MIKE GAUTHIER

CEFCOM had been created just as we were arriving in theatre. The
intent was to improve the way overseas operations are conceived, led
and supported. Mike ran CEFCOM, so I'd be talking to Mike a lot. He
had three jobs: to oversee the operation, to shape the conduct of the
mission over time with guidance from the CDS, and to work closely
with the army, navy and air force to make sure our men and women
deployed in harm's way had the tools to do what Canada was asking.
In short, his role was to provide clear guidance and orchestrate support
for the mission, leaving me and my successors free to execute that mission in response to changing circumstances on the ground.

I'd been focused on Afghanistan since 2002. I'd seen it evolve. I'd
been briefed by the U.S. three-star general Dan McNeill in Kabul

in June of 2003 (his chief of staff was a peppy guy named Stan McChrystal) who confided in me that the fighting in Afghanistan would all be over by January. Think about that: the corps commander of all U.S. troops in Afghanistan figured it would all be over within months. No criticism, but he was dead wrong because he, like us, could not have known the degree to which things would soon change.

MIKE GAUTHIER

Our mission was never conceived to be a conventional combat operation. We were there to conduct security operations, build the capacity of the Afghan security forces, and carry out reconstruction and development that would directly benefit Afghans themselves. We'd be doing all three of these things concurrently, or at least that's what we hoped. To channel Donald Rumsfeld, at that time none of us knew what we didn't know.

We did a recce in August of 2005, ready to undertake the mission as General Hillier had framed it, which was to go and build a nation. Our intent was always to help restore the country to its citizens. Canadians would be there to help Afghans take back control of their lives from usurpers who were intent on destroying their civil rights. So we landed in Kandahar ready to be the biggest—and most robust—provincial reconstruction team ever to hit Afghanistan. That's how we saw it. We were talking about simply using enough force to push the Taliban out of one village and town after another so that Afghan government forces could re-enter and provide the kind of support and stability that would rob the Taliban of their influence. At that time, counter-insurgency wasn't even a term we used, and most of us weren't comfortable later when some of us insisted on using it in our mission statements.

To be clear, Canada was never going into Afghanistan to kill bad guys. Even when things heated up and the Americans were pushing us to chase Taliban all over the place, and capture and kill as many as possible, we never once saw our mission that way. But it's true that when you sign up to a coalition and multinational operations, you have to allow for some give and take. It's the only way you'll be able to achieve all national and coalition objectives, which are often in conflict.

Coalition operations are ugly. The rule of thumb is that if you end up upsetting everyone, you've probably hit the sweet spot. In our case, as things would go from difficult yet possible to simply impossible, the pressure would come at us concurrently from national, international, U.S. and NATO interests. I decided early on that only when I had everybody screaming at me from all sides would I know I was doing a good job.

CHAPTER 3

LAND

The Boss told me that in times of conflict, leaders lead, and in between conflict, managers take over. There are senior people out there right now with zero operational experience.

Some of those clowns I wouldn't follow into a beer store.

MOTHER

W hen I arrived in Afghanistan in February 2006, I met the theatre commander for Operation Enduring Freedom, Lieutenant General Karl Eikenberry. Karl ran all U.S.-led coalition forces, of which our Canadian Task Force Aegis would now be a part. When I think of him now, two words come to mind: *no nonsense.* Our brigade appeared in theatre in February when Operation Enduring Freedom was still underway and fully five months before ISAF was scheduled to take over Regional Command South. On day one I and a handful of my senior staff were asked to attend a briefing Karl was to give at his headquarters in Kabul. When we got there, I sat with some thirty other officers at a conference table, but most of the conversation that day was between no one but Karl and me.

Right there in public, he grilled the crap out of me. He began by asking, "Is there anything you bring to this fight that will be in any way useful to me? I could have had any number of brigade headquarters, but I now have yours. Is there some advantage in that?" His interrogation was something right out of Nigel Hamilton's book *Monty: The*

Karl Eikenberry was the OEF theatre commander when we arrived. A highly intelligent and ener-getic officer, he commanded all OEF troops, including 10th Mountain Division and the U.S. special forces. I always went to his office or to briefings prepared for a grilling. When we arrived for our recce in late 2005, he asked us to attend one of his meetings with the Afghan authorities. He held a pre-meeting with his team to go over what the objectives were; and also a post-meeting, which he kicked off by asking, "What did we learn from that?" I liked Eikenberry because he was both smooth and demanding, and he also wanted to teach those around him. I saw that first when we briefed his staff on our incoming formation in Kabul. In a room of about thirty officers, he ques-tioned me for some time on what we could do, couldn't do, and determined the risk profile of this unknown formation. It was a very challenging meeting that was certainly a good introduction to how things would go. Eikenberry, along with the entire OEF team, was all business. They had been conducting combat operations for years and their members were very experienced. Eikenberry did not hold back on their concerns about the Canadians being merely peacekeepers or the unproven units within the brigade. At the time, it was a very unpleasant session; however, it was absolutely necessary for two reasons. One, OEF needed to understand what they were getting in terms of units and leadership. Two, it was our introduction to how business was to be approached and we realized we would have to pick up our game. Those first months under Eikenberry and 10th Mountain were invaluable to prepare us for Operation Medusa.

Making of a General, which details how Field Marshal Viscount Montgomery routinely grilled his commanders to ensure they knew what he needed them to know. Clearly Karl had read that book, because he sure as hell put me through the wringer. He proposed a number of scenarios, demanding to hear how we Canadians would respond should any of them occur. At one point he asked, "What will you do if attacked from out of Pakistan?" I answered that I would return fire for as long as it took to ensure my self-defence. He was more than satisfied with that. Later I let Ottawa in on the rule of engagement I had just conceived on the fly.

It appealed to me that General Eikenberry had the capacity to think of everything. I liked that. Each scenario he described was a likely event, so I was eager to offer my response and have it challenged. His interrogation stretched me. We worked through each scene in detail, refined our concept of operations in each case, and brainstormed how we might work under Operation Enduring Freedom and then under ISAF given the alarming spectrum of national caveats restricting our actions.

As Karl Eikenberry and I talked through each situation, we candidly discussed our capabilities and shortfalls. Most of our Canadian soldiers going to Afghanistan would have little other than United Nations experience under their belts. The last time our military saw combat was during the Korean War in the 1950s. It had therefore been ages since we had practised the skills that our American and British counterparts had lately exercised and refined in Iraq and Afghanistan. Our UN peacekeeping and peacemaking missions had taught us invaluable lessons, but not lessons in combat per se. Late in the 90s and in the early part of this century, Canada had begun participating in more robust NATO missions, but those too had not been combat missions. As such our learning curve would be steep for the first few months. We were re-learning how to conduct brigade operations in combat. That's why we faced such diligent interrogation from our American commanders when we first arrived.

The grilling was the first of many challenges I would encounter as general officer in command in Afghanistan, and I respected

Eikenberry for his forthright approach, a deep dive into almost every potential issue. In the end I seemed to have answered all his questions satisfactorily, and he knew what he could get from me and my brigade. When we were done he offered us more assistance in materiel and personnel than we would ever have thought possible.

The second commander I encountered in theatre was Major General Benjamin Freakley. With his 10th Mountain Division (Light Infantry), Ben was serving Operation Enduring Freedom as the division-level commander in charge of Combined Joint Task Force 76. I had met Ben twice before and was nervous to do so again, as both earlier encounters had not gone well. The previous summer, while preparing for Afghanistan, I had taken about twenty staff of my brigade headquarters to Fort Drum in upstate New York. We were there for a five-day command post exercise with the U.S. brigades we would soon join in theatre. The idea was that we in command would refine our procedures by working together in simulated combat situations.

Fort Drum was home base for the storied 10th Mountain Division, and had been established in the early 1800s to control smuggling between Canada and the United States on Lake Ontario and the Upper St. Lawrence River. As such, it was associated with a long history of wary suspicion between the two nations, a fact that would soon strike me as poetically appropriate.

Ben Freakley was running this exercise for his own divisional headquarters and was carefully assessing the readiness of the four brigades going with him to Afghanistan. We arrived with a detailed work plan in hand. On the first day I told my staff, "Go meet your cohorts and get to know them. These are the guys we're going to be working with over there. We'll regroup at the end of the day and compare notes." And off we went. I called on General Freakley, who was cordial and welcoming. It was the first time I had met him, and I liked him instantly. He introduced me to his chief of staff, who was also pleasant and upbeat. Knowing how closely we'd be working when I took command of RC South in February 2006, I was encouraged by their openness.

Two warrior generals: General Bismillah Khan Mohammadi, Chief of Staff of the Afghan National Army and Major General Ben Freakley, commander of the 10th Mountain Division and deputy commander of the ISAF. Both were cut from the same cloth because they had grit, never shied away from a fight and loved their troops. Bismillah Khan was in the field during Medusa almost every other day directing his troops. The terrain was not foreign to him because he was a Mujahideen fighter who had fought the Soviets many years earlier. It was good for everyone to see their commander out in the field taking charge of what at that time was Afghanistan's largest fight. Following Operation Medusa, Bismillah Khan told me that we had done what no other westerners had: fight and win against the defenders on the ground that had seen victories over Alexander the Great, the British and the Soviets. These are words that I will always cherish. Ben Freakley was also out as often as he could. Ben loved the field and talking to soldiers. Whenever he could, he and I would visit Omer Lavoie's unit and the other elements fighting around Kandahar. We maximized our visits, with Ben talking to the senior commanders and I to the company commanders. We verified what we were being told through various sources, assessed the situation on the ground from our troops in contact, and talked to locals throughout the fight.

Not for long, however. As the day rolled on I caught more than one reference to a U.S. brigade combat team out of Louisiana which was also supposedly going to take over RC South. As I knew that role was going to be taken by our Canadian brigade, not theirs, I assumed they had concocted a fictitious scenario for this command post exercise only. I was wrong.

> When I first took command of the 10th Mountain Division, I got read into the plan to deploy to Afghanistan for Operation Enduring Freedom. I was under the impression that our combined joint task force would consist of two manoeuvre brigades, an aviation brigade and a sustainment brigade. So four of the brigades I already commanded would be going to Afghanistan. I was unaware of the Canadian-led multinational brigade being considered on the troop list at that time.
>
> BEN FREAKLEY

So they had assumed we were just there for an exercise, no doubt thinking we were later going to play a different role somewhere else. Before the end of the day I went back to Ben's chief of staff and said, "This may be a stupid question, but you guys do realize we're coming to Afghanistan with you, right?" He did not. Moreover, he insisted we would not. I replied, "Ah, I think we have a problem here." By the time our brigade team regrouped, many of us had come to the same realization: "They don't know we're coming to Afghanistan." I phoned Ottawa and explained the situation.

We had no choice. That night we packed up and went home to Canada. All twenty of us.

We had been right, of course. We would be going. The unfortunate confusion at Fort Drum meant only that we did not get the chance to work alongside our U.S. partners before appearing in theatre. I long regretted that.

The next time I saw Ben Freakley was at our own command post exercise in Alberta in the late fall. He came to learn how we operated, and we were equally eager to see how he operated. Ours was to be an international brigade group, meaning that the team commanding Regional Command South would be composed of officers and troops from many different nations. But when Ben arrived many of those international partners hadn't even shown up yet.

> Commanding a brigade is hard. People don't realize that. When you are a battalion commander, you are expected to have an organization that's well-framed in the competency it delivers to the battlefield. So if you're infantry you're supposed to have a very coherent, well-trained infantry force. If you're artillery you're supposed to have a typically qualified, well-trained artillery force. But above those it's the brigade commander and his staff that become the orchestra conductors who have to know how to blend the capabilities of each of these pieces to a coherent and effective team. It's like a hockey coach who has to make sure the goalies, the defence and the front line that attacks all play as a team. And serve as a team. You have to train hard to do that well. The brigade training I observed in Alberta was really entry-level, clearly unappreciative of the complexities of regional command style. David didn't have his full team, that was my first concern. People he was supposed to have in his staff sections weren't there. And because they hadn't formed the team yet, there wasn't trust between the British chief of staff and the Canadians, which would be essential. The team was unformed. I went to my leadership and said, "They are not ready."
>
> BEN FREAKLEY

Ben Freakley wasn't our ultimate commander, of course. As I've said, until the turnover from U.S. forces to ISAF, Karl Eikenberry was the Operation Enduring Freedom commander we reported to after we arrived in February. After the turnover, David Richards would hold the top job in the coalition. So before and after, I could raise any concerns I had to someone senior if I had to, and sometimes I did. Freakley didn't think much of coalitions, and yes, he had come to the conclusion that we Canadians weren't ready for the challenges we had taken on. But once we were in theatre, he always listened and, perhaps because I was a Canadian, allowed me to push back more than any of his own subordinates could when an issue arose. Ben and I didn't often disagree, but when we did later over matters of operations, there was lots of yelling on both sides.

> I had a major argument with Lieutenant General Eikenberry. My view was that we should bring the third brigade, the fourth brigade, the aviation brigade and the sustainment brigade, and conduct operations in such a manner that the member nations of NATO would not have to fight their way into Afghanistan. There was already political friction around the commitment by NATO to come to Afghanistan. And the assumption, the horrible assumption made by NATO leaders and planners in Brussels, was that this was going to be a peacekeeping operation. It was not going to be a peacekeeping operation. In any intelligence that you had, in any open source that you read, in any awareness you had whatsoever, the Americans, the Germans, the Italians and others who were already in Afghanistan were fighting. They weren't enforcing peace, they weren't conducting a peacekeeping operation. They were fighting. It was combat. And I was clear with David from the beginning that he was coming to Afghanistan in a combat operation.
>
> BEN FREAKLEY

I had learned before we arrived that our Americans allies harboured a deep concern that we Canadians were about to enter combat on their behalf without being at all combat ready. I couldn't disagree. Two decades of peacekeeping cannot prepare an army for classic combat.

Peacekeeping, peacekeeping . . . When you raise a lieutenant to a captain to a major to lieutenant colonel to a whatever, and their training has been only in peacekeeping, and all their practical experience has been only in peacekeeping, and you then thrust them into a combat operation, it's like asking a cricket player to play football. So you have a mixed group of individuals who are in no way a coherent team. To use another metaphor, you have musicians who all have different sheets of music while the conductor is trying to get them to play one song.

BEN FREAKLEY

Ben Freakley was never shy about voicing an opinion. He was and is larger than life, strong as an ox with a personality to match. He is built like a football player and, like a football player, never took to the field with any thought other than victory. With decades of combat experience, he knew exactly what worked and what didn't. Part of that came from his significant experience planning for and executing big operations. He helped draft the war plans for Operation Desert Shield in the 1990s, later planned Operation Desert Storm with David Petraeus, then served as Chief of Infantry at Fort Benning, the base on which 120,000 U.S. troops each year are trained and made ready to deploy around the world. As both the head of Combined Joint Task Force 76 and the Deputy Commander Operations for ISAF in 2006, he was in Afghanistan to get hard things done.

We have a number of useful euphemisms in the army. One of them is the word *kinetic*. When you shoot people and blow things up, you are said to be in the "kinetic phase" of an operation. Freakley was a kinetic guy. He loved a fight and always wanted to be where the action was. For his insistence on rapid and aggressive offensive action, people routinely compared him to General George Patton, who once told his troops, "I don't want any messages saying 'I'm holding my position.' We're not holding a goddamned thing. We're advancing constantly and we're not interested in holding anything except the enemy's balls . . . There will be some complaints that we're pushing our people too hard. I don't give a damn about such complaints. I believe that an ounce of sweat will save a gallon of blood."

Freakley was tough on everyone, always in the pursuit of complete readiness for battle. Yet he was fair, honest, respectful of talent, open-minded and ready to learn. He worked hard to give those under him the assets they needed to succeed, a practice we would benefit from during Operation Medusa when he assigned us his own troops and air support to offset the unrealistic force ratios we faced going into battle.

Tension would arise from one other factor though. I suspect that Ben Freakley did not fully understand the complexity of our international activities in RC South and our whole-of-government approach. We had been sent there to stabilize a situation, aid a populace, help restore a society and give the governance of a democratic country back to its people. The last thing Rick Hillier had said to me before I headed to Afghanistan was, "Dave, build me a nation." When we wrote our operational plans, we defined our actions with verbs such as *secure*, *defend*, and only sometimes *defeat*. Freakley routinely went straight to the word *destroy*.

We weren't conducting warfare as he knew it, or even as he saw it happening in the less complex RC East, where his brigade commander John Nicholson was having a much easier time of it than we were. When Freakley advocated for immediate kinetic action, I countered by outlining the many competing priorities we faced. These included getting civilians to safety, using restraint to minimize collateral damage to people and structures, forwarding development activities as a way of securing the trust of the locals rather than just blowing up their villages to get at the Taliban, and dealing with all the restrictions that each of the various NATO nations had regarding how their troops could and could not be engaged. That kind of nuance just left Ben scratching his head.

In May he sent a team under Brigadier General James Terry from his division tactical headquarters at Bagram Airfield near Kabul to Kandahar. He wanted his own people to look in on our situation and

Rick Hillier was our Chief of Defence Staff and someone I had known for a while. A charismatic and visionary leader, he had an infectious aura—everyone liked him, as did I. He displayed tremendous trust in his people and allowed us to get on with it. This support, coupled with his good humour, made our job in Afghanistan that much more manageable. Hillier came over many times to visit the troops. What people saw in the photos in the papers were lots of laughs, but behind the scenes in one-on-one meetings we had serious discussions about everything to do with mission accomplishment, procurement timelines for essential equipment, etc. Hillier listened intently and ensured that we always had the support we asked for. At the end of his trip in March, he pulled me aside and said that he was staying on for a day and would attend the visit by Prime Minister Stephen Harper. This was a surprise to all of us. Rick was supposed to go on holiday with his wife and friends, but due to this visit he would not be able to. In typical Hillier fashion, he made a joke that his wife would understand but that it would cost him another trip somewhere down the road. Hillier was always able to lighten the mood. Following the transfer of authority to me as the commander of RC South, he looked at me and said, "You're on your own. Cheers!"

give him the truth. Terry subsequently reported back that we actually knew what we were doing and that the situation was indeed as difficult as reported, if not more so. That's when Ben Freakley concluded that he needed to assist more than insist.

Despite our differences, I learned more about being a general from Ben Freakley than from anyone else in my career. He is a man of deep convictions: religious, ethical and patriotic. Nothing he did was based on mere personal bias. No one before or since has displayed such tactical depth and such a strong desire to pass that knowledge on to others. Doctrinally driven and meticulous, he was the only commander over there ready and qualified to discuss the most minute details of plans at length. Given his endless appetite for the specific, it was no surprise to me that Freakley came right to Kandahar when it came time to put the plans for Operation Medusa through a rehearsal of concept drill. He wanted to be part of it.

CHAPTER 4

CONNECT

We had a big learning curve with the terminology. Suddenly we had to use American terms. For example, they say VSA, we say KIA. But whether it's "Vital Signs Absent "or "Killed in Action," you've still got the same problem.

MOTHER

As co-director of the Bi-National Planning Group in Colorado Springs from 2003 to 2005, I learned a ton about inter-agency cooperation. While its name was nondescript (read "boring"), the organization was responsible for coordinating joint foreign policy, defence and security approaches between the U.S. and Canada after the 9/11 attacks. Big stuff.

Back in 2002, it was obvious that an overarching vision for continental defence and security organizations was completely missing from the North American dialogue. The U.S. was reacting quickly and resolutely on its own—among other things, creating the United States Northern Command (USNORTHCOM). As a combatant command responsible for homeland security and defence, it was the first of its kind since the formation of the Continental Army in the time of George Washington. Canada decided not to get formally involved as we had with NORAD (the North American Aerospace Defense Command), but joint issues such as maritime domain awareness, support of civil authority, and intelligence sharing had to be coordinated, so the Bi-National Planning Group was born. Working alongside USNORTHCOM, we did everything NORAD didn't.

In my role as director, I worked with Americans on two questions: how to share critical intelligence in a post-9/11 world, and how to use our militaries to support civil authorities tasked with keeping citizens safe. One of our big successes was to change the habit of passing intelligence between Americans and Canadians from a need-to-know to a need-to-share basis. We knew that in a world of web-connected global terrorism, there would never again be time to figure out who needs to know something before that something explodes. The people you trust should get to see everything you have. With more qualified experts looking at more granular data, the likelihood of sniffing out and stopping terrorist plans would be greater. Since then, history has proved the wisdom of that approach many times over.

From the Americans I learned volumes about the dangers of thinking that any military can go it alone in hostile situations. Armed forces have centuries of experience standing up to other armed forces, but in the world of thugs, drug dealers, warlords, insurgents, arms merchants, bent politicians, corrupt businesses, bogus advocacy groups and fanatical anarchists such as Al-Qaeda, Boko Haram, Hezbollah, Lashkar-e-Taiba, Al-Shabaab, Hamas, Farc (I'm stopping for breath here), the Lord's Resistance Army, ISIS and the Taliban, a conventional military on its own has limited value. Most of today's battles are gang wars, so you better put people on your team who know how to fight them.

I had eye-opening conversations with senior officers in the Drug Enforcement Administration (DEA), the agency started by Richard Nixon in the early 1970s to stop the flow of drugs from places like Colombia. You don't have to watch *Narcos* on Netflix to know how that went. Despite an almost unlimited budget, no agency was able to stem the tide of illicit drugs onto the U.S. mainland, but there was an upside. The DEA learned a lot about the mistakes it made and is eager to share them with anyone going into a situation where drug money fuels a local or regional economy. Think Afghanistan and heroin.

The guiding principle in these situations is to connect with the community that has the problem. You can't start by shooting and arresting people. You must make human links based on respect and trust, and prove to the people you're trying to help that you can be of greater value to them than the thugs controlling them. Think thugs like the Taliban.

But who knows how to do this? Not the military. Not the diplomats. Not the NGOs. It's the police. Cops think differently than soldiers. They work a beat. They show up over and over. They get to know people. They help people. In time, people learn to trust them and they tell them things.

Human intelligence is an invaluable commodity. Coming out of my time in Colorado, that thought was top of my mind. So when I began planning for our rotation in Afghanistan, I knew we needed cops on the team. A talented police officer can tap into local knowledge and gather personal opinions about what is going on. So I began telling people that I was looking for police officers with community experience to be a part of my intelligence group. They could help collect information and analyze what it meant. We would then know what the local people knew, what they needed, what they were afraid of, and what they thought we should do first to contribute to their security.

I didn't have to look long. While we were still in Canada, someone said, "Oh, we have a policeman joining the team up in Kabul. His name is Harjit Sajjan. He works in Vancouver as both an army reservist and a policeman. And he does gangs."

Bingo.

I said, "Outstanding. But he's no longer going to Kabul; he's coming with me to Kandahar. I need a policeman, because the Taliban are nothing more than a bunch of thugs. He's the kind of guy I want." We met in Edmonton soon after.

Harjit was born in the Punjab, arriving in Canada when his parents came to seek a better life. In his teenage years he rode with a rough crowd, but found the courage to ditch some friends who were encouraging him to join a street gang. That decision shaped him. After that, he took pains to find ways to contribute to the community, later joining the militia with the British Columbia Regiment, the police with the

Vancouver Police Department's gang squad, and federal parliament in 2015 as the MP for Vancouver South. That same year he would be named as Canada's Minister of National Defence.

But in 2006 he was just a cop on a leave of absence from his department, serving his country as a soldier in Afghanistan. I admired him. We spoke about what I needed from him, and when he asked how things were going to work, I said, "We'll figure it out as we go along. But I need you to be working with my intelligence guys. You're a policeman. I need your police mentality to help my military intelligence guys understand the Taliban. They're not a formed army; they're thugs, a bunch of pick-up guys running an operation no different than the gangs you deal with in Vancouver." He agreed to join the team.

In March 2006 we had an important meeting with the Governor of Kandahar at the Tea House at Kandahar Airfield. I took Harjit Sajjan with me. Harj did not look like your average Canadian grunt, and the governor took an instant liking to him. While Afghans share a long border with Pakistan, that's relatively recent. Their hearts still lie with their historic neighbours in India. They are particularly fond of Sikhs, with whom they identify. Sikhs and Afghans are revered worldwide for their deep courage and notable success repelling invaders. They are both warriors at heart.

The governor's nod proved that Harj had broken down the first barrier. I made him our liaison with the governor's office from then on. But his greater task lay ahead. "You're a policeman," I said. "Go do community policing. There's your community — it's called Kandahar. Get to know the tribal elders and the people they trust. Get me information on what's going on from the Afghan point of view. Speak with my voice when you're out and report directly to me when you return."

Harj dug in. He started talking with everyone, and he was good at it. He got a whole bunch of information and reported it in substantial detail. The stuff he gathered was primary-source, from Afghans themselves. We compared that evidence with our other data sources. If all those sources said the same thing, then the raw data became actionable intelligence.

That's how, over time, we built situational awareness. Based on that awareness, we came up with plans to deliver the effects I was trying to achieve. Harj had helped us connect with the locals.

Another great source of local information was our padre, Captain Suleyman Demiray. Suleyman was born and educated in Turkey, graduating with his Master's in Theology from Ankara University. He emigrated to Canada in 1993. Ten years later, he became the first-ever

Everyone thinks mostly about the kinetic operations we conducted, whereas the majority of the time soldiers were interacting with the locals to establish relationships and deliver the things they wanted and needed. It took time to build these relationships because Afghans have seen so many foreigners and are justifiably distrusting. An understanding could only materialize after months of working with them, listening to them and most of all delivering real things (not just words). We never met with local villagers without doing our homework first and figuring out what they needed.

Muslim chaplain in the Canadian Armed Forces. When he headed with us to Afghanistan, he had intended to do the usual and simply serve our troops as a padre. But it occurred to me right away that Suleyman was the only guy in our entire brigade who could legitimately enter a mosque. Therefore I gave him specific orders: "Engage the Muslim leadership. Talk to the religious leaders, professors and elders and start building relationships with them. Show them we're here to listen and help. That's exactly why we're all here. I can make that point in local political circles, but I can't in religious circles. You can."

Like Harj had done, Suleyman jumped in with both feet. He started going into mosques and talking to people, and he accompanied us to meetings of every kind. I remember the day we opened up Forward Operating Base Martello, a Canadian outpost in the northern part of Kandahar. Padre Demiray was right there with us, and everyone in attendance was stunned. Really perplexed. Who was this guy? They knew the uniform, but inside it was a man who looked a lot more like them than any of our soldiers. And then he started to pray with them, in their faith, in their language. Amazing.

Once he did that, we had them. They rallied around and asked him where he was from. "Canada," he said. "I'm Canadian. I'm a proud Canadian. I'm a Muslim Canadian. And I'm in the Canadian Armed Forces. I want you to know that we're here to help you, we're here to work for you. Now what can we do?" And then he listened, over and over, until he learned things we never could have discovered without him there.

In early June in Kandahar, Suleyman met with Mawlana Abdul Samed, assistant director for Hajj and Awqaf, which means "Pilgrims and Trusts." Basically, he was the regional deputy of religious affairs — slated soon to become the director. Suleyman asked Samed what issues his team were struggling to overcome in the area. Samed offered some eye-opening insights. He reported that in the city of Kandahar there are two hundred mosques with the authority to offer Khutbah, the regular ceremony in the Islamic tradition of prayers and preaching that

Christina Green worked for the Canadian International Development Agency in Kabul. I heard about her from people in the development world and she was the professional we needed to build our sector development plan. It took tremendous effort to lure her away from Kabul and work for us in the dusty and under-developed south. Add to that fact, the necessity to work with soldiers who do not have the best of reputations for 'building' and she was very wary of our invite. After some time, she came onboard and I cannot say enough about what she did. She never gave us, the military, any quarter for what we did. She was like a fresh set of eyes questioning us and ensuring that we always had a development component to everything we did. Christina was good humoured and driven to help Afghans which added to our own credibility. She was connected with the development world and found resources we would have never found, and she produced plans and coordinated our efforts in the south that became a force multiplier of note. She was one of a kind as far as we were concerned.

typically falls on a Friday. At that time, only fifty of the imams who offered the Khutbah in those mosques were paid by the government, and the government was months late in paying them. So virtually every mosque in our region had to turn to its own congregation to fund the operation and maintenance of the facility and provide the meagre income of its imam. Few congregations could afford to pay. They needed a benefactor and one had stepped right up. The Taliban.

The Taliban were now routinely funding most of the mosques in Kandahar and the districts surrounding the city. Their money came with only one condition: the Taliban got to write the words spoken each week by the imams. In the campaign for hearts and minds, while we were dropping leaflets out of airplanes, the Taliban were preaching weekly to the faithful who were at the mosques to learn what was going on, what it meant, and how they as devout Muslims should respond. We weren't even allowed through the door. No wonder we were making so little headway.

Suleyman wrote a detailed report on the situation, and it rippled right up the chain of command. No one had suspected that the Taliban were entrenched at that level. The Americans had been in this country for over four years and never suspected. Thanks to our padre, we were able to make some sweeping recommendations, including that the salaries of all religious teachers and imams be paid directly by the Minister of Hajj and Religious Affairs, that training centres be established to re-educate local religious figures in the legitimate articles of the Islamic faith rather than the Taliban propaganda in which they'd been steeped, that religious inspectors and intelligence officers move out into the rural communities to rediscover what the true needs were, and that imams and mullahs who served their communities without Taliban influence be paid bonuses. The proposals were accepted. As Rick Hillier had hoped, we were beginning to help the Afghans rebuild their nation.

Once these recommendations had been made I told the padre that I had good news and bad news: "The good news is your work is having a deep positive effect. The bad news is you're not finishing your tour. You're staying here with me." Looking back, I could have used a hundred guys like him. He was a model Canadian—conciliatory, inclusive, attentive, caring. He didn't send messages to people; he related to them. He participated in an honest exchange of ideas. Nothing less was required, because Afghanistan is a nation of countless cultures and factions, a male-dominated society shaped by fifteen centuries of war.

The Afghans have an unbelievable traditional and historic culture. They have thrown off their oppressors many times—with British occupations in the 1800s, the Russians in the 1980s. They are very fiercely independent people, even tribe by tribe, and those tribes are not for the most part cooperative with one another. There are great rifts over who's got power and who's got control. There is a great east–west oblong area heavily occupied by the Pashtuns that extends across Kandahar, Uruzgan, Helmand, and well into Pakistan, which people sometimes call Pashtunistan. You have the Hazaras, mostly out of Bamyan Province, who are looked upon as sort of the lowest caste of this society. They seem to be pragmatic, hardworking people. You have the Tajiks out of Panjshir Province who are fierce fighters and had the relationship with Ahmad Shah Massoud, who ran the Northern Alliance and fought the Russians and the Taliban and was killed by Al-Qaeda. The Tajiks draw their strength from a tight-knit community in the Panjshir Valley, which, because of its high mountains and limited passes, is a sanctuary for the Tajiks. Very hard to get into, so there hasn't been a lot of fighting there. You can then add in the Uzbeks. All these tribes are like small nation states. They cooperate when to do so is in their best interests, and they don't when they can't see an advantage. Their culture is hard to understand. Even if we were there for a hundred years, we probably wouldn't get the culture right trying to figure out all the tribal and elder hierarchies, and who sways the people.

BEN FREAKLEY

The tribal dynamics alone were more complex than anything I'd seen in my twenty-five years in the military. Seeing those affiliations at work, we began to appreciate that there was much more going on than either our reports or our maps could convey. I asked to see an additional tribal map, and immediately we began to sense how the locations of particular tribes could help us predict patterns of social behaviour. This growing understanding of the human geography of the region significantly enhanced our assessment of what was and was not happening. We could have just gone out and killed people, but that wasn't anywhere near our mission. For one thing, for every guy you kill you create ten new insurgents, so military force alone would have been useless. We needed to understand people, side with them, train them, and help them build the capacity to sustain a better life.

Our soldiers knew that instinctively. The idea of helping locals develop vocations by which they could profit was motivating, and many of our men and women made a habit of using their downtime to teach Afghans marketable skills such as carpentry, metalwork, and electrical installation and maintenance. They would pitch in on building projects with families in Kandahar, bringing boxes full of tools and leaving a few of those tools behind as gifts. In a way, this activity was provincial reconstruction at its best—and reconstruction, after all, was a priority for us.

Sometimes, the contributions made by individual Canadian soldiers had deep and lasting impact on the whole country. I learned only recently, for example, that Major Rick Goodyear, a National Command Element comptroller who joined us midway in our tour, arrived at the idea that a change in the way banking was done could help the Afghan economy in important ways.

In August 2006, I deployed to Kandahar, Afghanistan as the Task Force Comptroller. When I arrived NATO nations were making 85 per cent of all their vendor and contractor payments in American dollars. In my experience, a currency is part of a country's fabric, something that citizens associate with their national identity. The

American dollar was the currency of choice and its prevalence was undermining the credibility of the native currency, the Afghani.

One of the common problems with any developing nation is that it takes a long time, sometimes decades, to establish the credibility of their currency, especially after a major conflict. Within a month of arriving in theatre I drafted a policy that all Canadian Forces personnel engaging in contracting and pro-curement in Afghanistan would make their payments in Afghani whenever possible.

The next objective was to get other nations to adopt the policy as well. I chaired a regular meeting of all the major con-tributing nations' finance officers. I outlined the rationale behind making payments in Afghani and convinced all the troop-contributing nations to adopt the same policy. There was an initial concern about whether or not there would be enough Afghani to use, but the truth is that no one had ever checked or asked. It was not an issue. The Afghans were quite willing and capable to provide the cash we needed.

Previous to this initiative, the majority of troop-contributing nations were also importing U.S. dollars from outside the country to pay contractors. This left the Afghan government with little to no ability to monitor the inflow and outflow of foreign currency. Restoring public faith in the Afghani would be an essential step to restoring faith in the credibility of the central bank and in government institutions.

Tackling the currency issue from another means, I enforced a rule that all vendors that Canada dealt with had to acquire bank accounts. That would ensure electronic records of all our financial transactions occurring in Afghanistan. Again, I presented the policy to my troop-contributing nation partners and it was adopted by all. Prior to this, the government had no means of knowing how much vendors were making or what they were doing with the money. Black market activity was rampant. The existing banks in the country were all signatories to international anti–money laundering protocols. Protocols that provided a measure by which the Afghan government could now monitor suspicious transactions.

Enforcing the need for vendors and corporations to adopt bank accounts and allowing the government visibility as to how much the businesses were earning also gave the government a means to collect taxes. Vendors could no longer hide revenues. From a nation-building perspective, Afghanistan needed all the help it could get to monitor revenues and cash flow and create a tax base. Without the knowledge of who was making what, it would have been nearly impossible to collect taxes and ultimately fund government programs. They weren't going to get much from poor farmers but there were corporations making lots of money in Afghanistan and, from my perspective, they should have been paying their share of taxes to help the country rebuild.

The adoption of bank accounts by our vendors also made life a little safer and more secure for Canadian troops and the Afghan vendors with whom we interacted. By using bank accounts, we didn't need to physically transfer millions of dollars of cash to pay a vendor. Transactions could now be done electronically and safely, with the government having oversight and reducing black market activity.

Once both policies were adopted, nearly 80 per cent of all payments effected in Kandahar province by all troop contributing nations were in Afghani and were completed electronically to a bank account.

RICK GOODYEAR

There was so much we could do. The damage to infrastructure in and around Kandahar was not just a result of the fight against the Taliban under Operation Enduring Freedom. The bulk of the destruction had happened after 1992 when the pro-Soviet communist regime finally fell.

At that time, all but one political party in the country agreed to share power and live in peace under the government of the Islamic State of Afghanistan, which was established by the Peshawar Accord of that year. The dissenter was Hezbi Islami, a party originally formed in 1975 and now subscribed to by many Pashtun students who had played a strong role in defeating the Soviets. They wanted an end to tribal rivalries and the establishment of a single non-ethnic regime. While these aims seemed identical to those of the government, Hezbi Islami reacted violently against the new Islamic State of Afghanistan. Between 1992 and 1996 they attacked government offices in and around Kabul. As Human Rights Watch has reported, "shells and rockets fell everywhere." The result was a civil war that shook the country, and from which Kandahar eventually suffered more than any other city, becoming what the Afghanistan Country Study Guide called "a centre of lawlessness, crime and atrocities fueled by complex Pashtun tribal rivalries."

Amid the chaos, warlords seized initiative in various parts of the country, paying for mercenaries, weapons and ammunition with the profits of poppy and marijuana production. They turned the civil war into a gangland turf war. Oddly it was their abuse of power—notably the systematic raping of children—that led another group of students, under Mohammed Omar, to form the Taliban and go after them. Once again, it was war. The destruction continued.

Mullah Mohammed Omar was a shy, quiet, private man. An ethnic Pashtun, he was born poor sometime after 1950 in Kandahar Province, in a village reported by many (but not all) to be in the Panjwayi District. Omar's subsequent rise to leadership, power and celebrity gave his Panjwayi home special significance to his followers, in time distinguishing the area as the so-called heartland of the Taliban. Whether deserved or not, it led his disciples to a conviction that dying for their cause in Panjwayi would be selfless and noble, much as modern soldiers feel about sacrificing their own lives to save their comrades in arms. A more cynical view of the heartland theory holds that because Panjwayi land is fertile, it is therefore profitable.

Most of the Taliban now own property there. Looking for the Taliban? Follow the money.

It's tough for westerners observing the atrocities of the Taliban to comprehend how such perversion of logic could attract any followers at all, let alone the tens of thousands who have sacrificed their lives to the cause. The secret may lie in the Taliban's distinct approach to the provision of security services, and to appreciate that you have to understand zakat.

In Islamic tradition, zakat is a form of tithing by which the faithful share their wealth with others. As one of the Five Pillars of Islam, zakat is considered in many nations to be a sacred and purifying obligation rather than just a personal act of charity. The amount given to the community depends on each person's income and total wealth, and is typically calculated as a percentage, often 2.5 per cent or one-fortieth of someone's total situation. The Taliban were well aware of the exact percentage members of each community were comfortable paying. When they demanded payment for security, they set their protection fee no higher than that familiar percentage, knowing it would at least appear as reasonable. They then protected their new clients by intimidating any would-be aggressor. In great part, that's why the Taliban are tolerated.

> Local government leaders, corrupt members of the Karzai government, and warlords might say, "We'll do your security for 20 per cent," or perhaps 15 per cent, but in any case at a much greater rate than the Taliban ever did. The Taliban did everything consistently with the religious norms and cultural experiences of the Afghan people. That's both how they recruited and how they swayed people with an alternative view, saying, "Hey, NATO can't secure you, and the Afghan government can't secure you, and most of the Afghan army and the Afghan police can't secure you, but we can. We'll fight for your tribe, protect you against the other tribes, and we'll do that for only the amount you're already paying at the mosque." Given that argument, if you were someone in that

situation wouldn't you be more likely to trust somebody who speaks your language, lives amongst you, practises your religion, is culturally adept at interweaving themselves into your society? Or would you be inclined to trust some other guys from the outside that are very foreign to you? Remember these are people with a 22 per cent literacy rate. We in the West don't fully appreciate the power of education. Sitting in *shuras* [decision-making sessions] on mountaintops with some of these Afghan people, we saw them react to a helicopter, a jet airplane, an armoured vehicle from Canada as something from outer space. If you've lived with a wheelbarrow and a hoe most of your life, even a bulldozer showing up in your area will seem extremely foreign. But when you look at a guy walking into your village with an AK-47 and a blanket, wearing the same hat you wear, speaking your language, you will be more drawn to that person, even if he's a Taliban. It's an issue of trust following familiarity.

The worst form of leadership is intimidation, and it's practised brutally by the Taliban. By the late 2000s the Taliban were taking women who had been raped into soccer stadiums, tying them to posts and publicly executing them in front of 8,000 people for being promiscuous. If you did not conform to the Taliban way, you were going to be treated with the most extreme forms of violence, and that served as a deterrent to the rest of the population whom they wished to control. But people have short memories. By the mid to late 2000s people had forgotten. That's true even today. People make trades. Who do they think is the better angel to engage: the Taliban or coalition forces? That depends on how they've been treated themselves.

BEN FREAKLEY

A casual look at a fundamentalist, fanatic, misogynist regime that has routinely stoned women to death for adultery, beheaded enemies, armed children with explosive devices, dragged farmers in front of firing squads for "colluding" with the government, and who famously allowed Osama bin Laden to operate his Al-Qaeda training camps in Afghanistan and then refused to turn him over after 9/11, will inspire little sympathy. While the lazy conclusion that the Taliban are just evil is momentarily satisfying, it is unhelpful in the long run. While power routinely corrupts, the corrupt seldom achieve power through brute force alone. They either start out with a sincere vision of a better future that appeals to the masses, or they fake it. In Mohammed Omar's case, the original call to arms was made in reaction to widespread abuse of the Afghan poor by the opportunists who seized power in the vacuum created when the Russian invaders were finally expelled from Afghanistan in 1989.

Seventeen years later, we were there to help clean up the mess.

In the tenuous stability made possible by NATO intervention after 2004, our coalition of thirty-seven NATO nations had agreed that provincial reconstruction would be part of every campaign plan. We had to help the country rebuild its infrastructure. Leading RC South, Canada would have the job of making that happen around Kandahar. We knew that mission success would depend on far-reaching development activities as well as kinetic operations. So when we put together the Canadian team for Afghanistan in late 2005, I asked Rick Hillier to get me a policy advisor and a development advisor from Foreign Affairs. That seemed to me in line with the whole-of-government approach prescribed by the Canadian government itself. Rick set up a meeting, and I came in to brief Foreign Affairs on our campaign plan. Then I asked for their help. They did not look happy about that, and I sensed that interdepartmental collaboration was neither a strength nor an interest. Once again I asked for a policy advisor and a development advisor. We got the first in Pamela Isfeld. We did not get the second.

Without a policy advisor, we would have been hamstrung. With our deliberately chosen approach, we had to advance ambitious plans on three fronts at once: defence, diplomacy and development. So when

Pamela joined she was bolted right into our day-to-day operations, providing the context and expertise we needed to collaborate with the political world. She helped balance the interaction between us and Foreign Affairs, National Defence and the Canadian International Development Agency (CIDA), and became an important interface for the teams from other nations working in RC South. Pamela is a professional of great humility. Working with us she had to be; she got no special treatment, was quartered in the most modest digs imaginable, wore the same heavy and hot protective gear we all did, rode overland in dusty vehicles, walked on long patrols, and sat for countless meetings with Afghan authorities to help build relationships. She dug into her duties like a trooper, which everyone appreciated, and she had a solid sense of humour, which she often needed. I recall visiting Governor Armand in Zabul Province and taking Pamela along. Armand was a marvellous man—one of the best leaders Afghanistan has produced. He was walking us through a market in Qalat and, as we were strolling, casually grabbed a scarf for Pamela and said, "A gift from us." While our Afghan hosts never forced their culture on us, there was an unspoken hope that when out among the people whose help we relied on, we would be sensitive to the context. Pamela didn't miss a beat; she accepted the governor's gift with a smile and cheerily put the scarf on her head.

Pamela's role with us in the south of Afghanistan was new to Canada, and I felt for her as she worked out the arrangements with our ambassador in Kabul. Unnecessarily, Foreign Affairs had insisted that Pamela report back to them directly in Ottawa instead of to the ambassador—who, after all, was the head of mission. That made things awkward from time to time, but Pamela navigated those shoals and kept our work moving. We had the policy advisor we needed.

We still had no development advisor, however. When we arrived in theatre, we could see that the Americans were handling the development issue in their usual way, which was "big." To manage reconstruction, they had put together a massive operation in which most U.S. government departments were represented in some way. The United States Agency for International Development (USAID) led the effort, and when the 10th Mountain Division opened a door for us to the vast U.S. resources supporting their work, we linked up with USAID immediately. But with no Canadian development advisor to run our operation, we simply couldn't be effective even with their help. So we went on the hunt.

We had heard good things about a CIDA rep working out of Kabul named Christina Green. I reached out to her, and we had several conversations in which I proposed she come down and run things for us. She was a hard nut to crack; not easily convinced that we were ready to do big things, and even if we were she wasn't sure how she would fit in. I said she would work with me and lead all the development work for our region. Still she was not convinced. Over time I was able to walk her through our well-considered campaign plan, which detailed an operation whose success depended as much on community reconstruction and development as it did on fighting the Taliban. Eventually, she agreed.

Christina was everything our team was looking for: inquisitive, energetic, thorough, professional and engaging. She was indispensable to our work. She knew everyone in the overseas development world, where a vast network of professional allies stood by to help her out. People respected and trusted her, and she made important connections for us with the provincial reconstruction teams (PRTs) in each of the other provinces, with national agencies such as USAID, and with the more than thirty organizations running development projects in the Kandahar area. She was good-natured and easy to work with, but in no way a pushover. She held her own against suits and soldiers alike, and she fought against bureaucracy both in and out of theatre. Because of Christina, we never got bogged down. We did a lot and we did it fast.

In the summer of 2006 alone, we authorized and spent around 30 million dollars on reconstruction and development, of which two-thirds was funded by the U.S. We had negotiated a deal with USAID and had ready cash for discretionary spending, as do all U.S. commanding officers in the field. No longer did we have to wait for funding to be approved in Kabul and to trickle down like molasses through the usual channels. Whenever I and all my captains, lieutenants and sergeants set out to meet with elders, we made sure to arrive with pockets full. Need a pump? We'll fund that. Looking for a tractor? We have five outside. Trying to find something tougher to source? We'll deliver it tomorrow. Building a new village market? Here's two thousand in cash. At every turn, we proved that we were ready to work with them and that we could be trusted. We built relationships, and we showed them we knew how to do more than fire guns. And Christina ran it all.

We built schools, district centres and family dwellings, teacher training centres, hospitals and clinics. We dug 100 kilometres of irrigation canals, 150 kilometres of roads, erected four bridges, brought forty-two new generators online, dug 1,061 wells, laid 3 kilometres of water-supply pipes, ran sixteen vocational training courses and gave out 166 sewing machines and a large number of other tools.

With our growing knowledge of the needs of the locals, we knew what the priorities were. We were building, not killing. And every time we paved a road, we made it almost impossible for the Taliban to plant and hide IEDs in that road. Farmers could get their products to market, commerce could flow, people could get together to meet. With a secure road to travel and a district centre in which to gather, the three arms of Afghan civil society could get on with their business: the federal government with its money, the tribes with the people's authority, and the security forces with their protection.

Admittedly the Taliban went to great efforts to destroy anything we built, but that backfired on them every time. We would just go to the community and say, "Look, we built that thing together and the Taliban destroyed it. Your issue is now with them, not us." After these events it became apparent to each community that the Taliban was setting them back years in development. Meanwhile they saw first-hand the benefits of our help. Their teachers had had nothing but tents before; now they had schools, and literacy rates were climbing.

They'd had to travel miles for medical treatment before; now they had clinics, and mortality rates were falling. Their children had been dying of preventable diseases before; now they were inoculated, and contagion rates for measles and polio were at an all-time low. Their crops had been rotting in the fields before; now there were roads to take their produce to market, and there was more cash in their pockets. Every

Our medics were heroes every day. Their main task was to support our soldiers when the need was there. Tragically, they were some of the busiest people in Afghanistan. Everyone wanted to see them, knowing that they were there and that they were well trained, well equipped and supported by medevac and hospitals. With that knowledge, the men and women who went downrange threw themselves at every task knowing they would be cared for. Our medics also did a lot to help the local population. We often conducted medical outreach visits to villages. We would treat ill and injured Afghans either there in the villages or by taking them to our own hospitals. In this way we showed that we weren't just talk—we were actively providing much-needed medical care that otherwise was not available. And we did our utmost to be culturally sensitive to the needs of Afghans. We enlisted the aid of female soldiers to augment our female medics as they gave medical assistance to Afghan women and children. In this way, we proved repeatedly that our value sprang from much more than just fighting.

time we did something together, it made a difference. And every time the Taliban ripped something down, they proved that their only interest was self-interest. Their claim to be the only protectors of the people had less and less effect.

I am in no way holding up these results as some kind of long-term victory. A decade later, many of the villages we backed once again face conditions as bad or worse than they suffered then. The eventual failure of coalition nations to keep funding flowing provided fuel for the

The children in Afghanistan were wonderful. They were inquisitive when we walked around, and soldiers always had pencils on them because that is what the kids asked for. Education was the key to success, and was fundamental to helping the Afghan people. The children wanted to learn, as did their parents. School supplies were the one thing we asked Canadians to send over. They were always well placed. The other thing we did when we were out there was to help children and women with medical outreach visits. When women turned up without their children, we feared the worst.

Taliban propaganda machine. In addition, in our efforts we made a fatal mistake by leading with the military instead of the police. The immediate advantages of that approach were obvious: whenever we did something for a community, they protected us from attack, either by refusing to help the Taliban or by tipping us off to a threat. But no one is ever truly comfortable with an occupying force, even when it's there at the express request of one's elected government. It is the police, not the military that communities associate with law and order, even when some members of that police force may be corrupt. We blew that, and by "we" I mean our regional command, our entire NATO coalition, and the government of Afghanistan.

But I remember doing one thing right. Having learned the value of partnerships while working alongside (but not directly in) NORTH-COM in Colorado Springs, I looked around in Afghanistan for as many partners as I could find. Sometimes, however, they just appeared. In mid-June, Rick Hillier and I were just about to fly from Kandahar down to Mirage air base near Dubai, when we received an invitation from Mohammed bin Zayed bin Sultan Al-Nahyan, Crown Prince of Abu Dhabi, to join him at his mother's palace. His mother is Fatima bint Mubarak Al Ketbi, a vocal advocate for women's rights in the Arab world and a champion of educational reform. Like his mom, Al-Nahyan is a social progressive with a passionate interest in education, economic development and environmental protection. He is also Deputy Supreme Commander of the United Arab Emirates Armed Forces. The Emirates already had a small team in Afghanistan, and the prince was eager to learn more about what was going on over there. So when he heard we'd be in the area, he asked us over. We accepted and headed to the palace a day or two later. We were warmly received, and as someone brought in coffee and dates, Rick sat on one side of our host and I sat on the other.

Being a soldier himself, the prince asked what we were up to. So I told a bunch of war stories that illustrated what we were doing over there. It was a grand old talk, just three soldiers chatting. At the end, he leaned forward and said, "What can I do for you? What can we, the Emirates, do for you?" I was floored and put slightly on the spot, but in a moment I suggested that assistance in reconstruction might be ideal. "You can put up mosques," I said. Without radios and televisions, their mosques were the people's only source of information beyond gossip. But many mosques had been damaged in the civil war, and most had not been repaired or funded since. "I can't fix or build mosques," I told him. "I'm a Christian, but if you could do some of that, starting with the main mosque in downtown Kandahar, you would probably be really helpful." The prince just said, "Thank you very much for coming; it was a pleasure to see you," and ushered us out. This time I knew I didn't know what had just gone on. We headed back to Kandahar.

Two days later, three guys showed up in my office. Frankly, I don't even know how they found it. They said, "We've been sent by the Crown Prince. We're here to help you and we have a blank cheque to do so, but there are two conditions you must agree to. First, you may not tell anyone we're here. We'll just go about our business and do everything behind closed doors. We don't want any recognition. Second, once we start, you'll never hear from us again and you must not try to make contact." Good opener.

I said I could do that. I then contacted the Governor of Kandahar and said I had some people wanting to talk to him about reconstruction. He said he'd invite the tribal elders. As soon as we walked in, they all looked at my guests and fell off their chairs. The U.A.E. has huge gravitas in the region, and the Emiratis had just shown up. They all fell to chatting, and at one point the Emiratis and the governor just kind of turned to me and said they would take it from here. I never contacted them again. But I knew I had played a small role in getting one regional power to help another in a useful way; bringing a solution to this horrid conflict closer than any gun ever could.

Later, after my tour in Afghanistan, I paid a visit to my former OEF commander Lieutenant General Karl Eikenberry, in Brussels. Karl asked, "What are you doing tomorrow for breakfast?" The next morning, he introduced me to Richard Holbrooke, a special emissary to Afghanistan sent by Barack Obama to figure things out. Holbrook asked, "What should we be doing in Afghanistan?" I didn't hesitate. "Go get the Emiratis to help you. We can do a lot of stuff, but they can do it better. They think of the Afghans as brothers and sisters." And then I paraphrased T.E. Lawrence: "It's far better for people to do something imperfectly themselves than for anyone else to do something perfectly for them."

I learned that in Afghanistan.

CHAPTER 5

TRANSFER

We were led by some of the toughest, meanest men and women
in the CAF. I'm so lucky and proud to have served.

MOTHER

Briefing visitors from afar was part of our daily routine in
Afghanistan. Everyone wanted to know what was going on, and
the best way to find out was to come and talk to the men and
women on the front lines. Senior Canadian military officers, such as our
chief of defence staff Rick Hillier and our CEFCOM commander Mike
Gauthier, clearly had a pressing need to come and take the pulse, but
some visitors took us by surprise. In March 2006 when Rick was wrapping up one of his short stopovers in Kandahar, he pulled me aside to
announce that he was extending his stay by twenty-four hours so that he
could be with us to welcome Canada's prime minister, Stephen Harper,
who would then remain with us for three full days.

It was not uncommon for leading elected officials of NATO nations
to drop in and speak to their troops in theatre, but only for an hour or
two. A stop of three days by a prime minister was unheard of. It was also
a security risk. We coordinated the visit with 10th Mountain Division
and OEF through their headquarters at Bagram Air Base north of Kabul.
Mightily impressed by this clear demonstration of Canada's commitment to the mission, our American commanders perked right up and
gave us full support. Whatever questions they had about our intentions
were now going to be answered by the prime minister directly.

Prime Minister Harper came to visit the contingent in March 2006 for three days and two nights. This floored the coalition partners, as they were used to senior leaders coming in for a few hours —or maybe a day max. Our U.S. coalition partners in particular were astounded that he stayed as long as he did. The visit did an awful lot of good, dispelling some of the doubts about Canada's commitment to the mission in Afghanistan. Mr. Harper certainly impressed us with his intellect, and he was truly interested in seeing for himself what the situation was. We learned very quickly that PowerPoint presentations were less effective than just walking and talking with the boss, and showing him firsthand what was what. The troops loved seeing the PM and everyone wanted to get in a photo with him. At first the PM's staff set out to manage every aspect of the visit, and we had to tell them that security was ours to deal with and so any attempt to keep vehicles with guns out of the shots was ridiculous. After negotiation, we agreed to work together. The visit had a tremendous effect on the morale of the troops—and I think it had a significant impact on Mr. Harper as well. He got unvarnished opinions, which I gather he appreciated. Here the PM is touring the National Support Element (NSE) lines. The unit's commanding officer, Lieutenant Colonel John Conrad, can be seen over the right shoulder of Mr. Harper with John's regimental sergeant major, Chief Warrant Officer Eastman, on the PM's left side. John provided the Canadian contingent with all its administrative and logistical support. The NSE were the unsung heroes in Afghanistan. This was perhaps the best supported mission I have ever been on, in large part thanks to the logistics by John and his team.

Stephen Harper arrived the next day with an entourage of Ottawa-based bureaucrats intent on managing every aspect of the tour as if it were going down in Ottawa or Toronto. We had to advise them that there were overriding operational restrictions dictating what they could and could not do. After some butting of heads, we all took our appropriate roles and fell into a good routine that served each of our purposes.

Our troops were pumped to see their prime minister up close. The sight of hundreds of soldiers crowding the PM, peppering him with questions and squeezing in for selfies was something to behold. I was heartened to see that the PM was equally enthusiastic and really enjoyed engaging with Canada's front-line men and women. The Posse, not wanting to let such an opportunity slip by, asked if we too could get a photo with the boss. That shot remains for each of us one of the great mementos of the tour.

Over the next three days, Prime Minister Harper proved his keen interest in every aspect of the mission, while we learned that using PowerPoint is the worst way to brief a knowledgeable visitor. We quickly moved away from slides, preferring instead to hunch over tables and work with actual maps as we discussed the complex and unfolding situation in the southern part of Afghanistan for which we were responsible. We followed those briefings with extensive tours around camp and many dozens of ad hoc interactions with our troops. This unexpected and welcome visit boosted our morale and proved both to Canadians and to our partners in theatre that Canada was engaged and committed. That was helpful, because many people doubted that we and our NATO coalition were up to the task.

When NATO took over responsibility for the south of Afghanistan on July 31, 2006, most Afghans and Americans in military-diplomatic circles were hugely skeptical that NATO was even remotely ready for the challenge. Some of that doubt was warranted, in that NATO had little experience in actual combat, but much of the concern stemmed from bruised American pride. The U.S. had come into Afghanistan with a furious resolve to get the thing done. They had dedicated troops and equipment on a scale that no other nation could. But they had not accomplished their objectives, and the war in Iraq was beginning to consume more and more of their attention and resources. In a pivotal conversation at the time of the Istanbul Summit in June 2004, U.S. President George W. Bush had openly asked British Prime Minister Tony Blair for help in Afghanistan. Ever since, NATO had been preparing to take over.

During our five months with Operation Enduring Freedom under Lieutenant General Karl Eikenberry and the 10th Mountain Division, NATO had begun planning in earnest for the transition of operational responsibility to the new International Security Assistance Force (ISAF). ISAF was itself commanded by NATO's Allied Rapid Reaction Corps (ARRC), which reported up the chain of command to the Supreme Allied Commander Europe (SACEUR). Sorry about all the acronyms.

As commander of Regional Command South under OEF, I had been given responsibility for American troops. This clearly demonstrated that the United States trusted its relationship with Canada, and it also explained the grilling we received from all American commanders. They were making sure we were ready to command their troops in battle.

In May 2006, the commander of ARRC—a British Army lieutenant general named David Julian Richards—became the commander of ISAF as well. As such, when operational responsibility for the south of Afghanistan moved from OEF to ISAF on July 31, I would no longer be reporting as Commander RC South to Ben Freakley and Karl Eikenberry. David Richards would be my boss.

I knew David by reputation. Most did. As a brigadier in 2000 he had commanded Operation Palliser during Sierra Leone's civil war. His original mission there had been to go in with members of the 1st Battalion, Parachute Regiment (1 PARA) of the United Kingdom's Special Forces Support Group and rescue British foreign nationals from the capital city, Freetown. Yet when the situation on the ground escalated rapidly, David took the initiative and, with a pathfinder unit, led the defence of Freetown in a series of bloody firefights against the Revolutionary United Front. The ensuing political backlash painted the

David Richards was the commander of the Allied Rapid Reaction Corps when he was assigned to become the commander of ISAF. A British officer of some note, having made his name in East Timor and Sierra Leone, he was gregarious, charismatic, knowledgeable and inclusive. We were still working under Operation Enduring Freedom when he arrived, and he began our transition work immediately. We met several times early on and truly hit it off. David had his hands full leading NATO in its largest role outside of its normal geographical confines. He made Ben Freakley his deputy, which was an outstandingly wise choice. It ensured a close relationship with the Americans and gave him access to someone who understood the complexities of the situation, since he was the outgoing commander who had overseen both RC South and RC East. David's support of us at the tactical and operational level was unequivocal, especially during the planning of Medusa. Little to no support was coming from NATO. Regardless, David provided me with all the political top cover I needed in order to focus on the fight. I thoroughly liked working with him. He would ask the hard questions but he was always easy to work with. We remain good friends to this day. He took much pressure off us and addressed the NATO restrictions as much as he could.

brigadier as having acted beyond his authority, but we soldiers knew that David had done the right thing. Five years earlier the failure of another general to act similarly in Srebrenica had resulted in the massacre of 8,000 innocent civilians.

When I first met David Richards, I liked him immediately. He was charismatic and genuine. He was also an engaged commander who proved over and over that no task was too hard, no problem too thorny. As we would soon experience, David would make time for me and my team no matter how much he had on his plate. Given the complexity of operations ongoing at the transition, a lesser relationship would have been catastrophic to what we were doing on the ground at the time. And given the confusion within the NATO coalition, I'm not sure a lesser soldier could have made it work. The turnover wouldn't be easy.

As July 31 approached, there was considerable skepticism in Afghanistan amongst the Americans. I was aware of it probably more than others because I met a lot of senior Afghans and senior Americans, and I could tell that while they weren't openly opposed, their egos had been dented by the fact that a Brit was about to be commanding Americans at theatre level, which I was told was only the first time since the Second World War. They knew that NATO member nations would be more constrained by political and ethical considerations than they ever had been. European nations hadn't shown much muscle or spunk in decades, and the Americans were doubtful that these fighting units had been sufficiently hardened—which, without doubt, the Americans were. They sort of thought the British and Canadians would be all right, but they fully knew we had woefully too-few troops for what we were being asked to do, which was far more than they had ever undertaken.

DAVID RICHARDS

David, Karl and Ben shared one opinion, however. To be successful, they needed soldiers who were able to do the job. They had admired the skill of Lieutenant Colonel Ian Hope, our PPCLI battalion commander who had led Task Force Orion, but that group was now leaving to make way for Omer Lavoie and his Task Force 3-06. All three generals were now concerned that the Canadians taking on RC South were too new, too inexperienced, too soft.

> Battle-hardened troops are different. There's a look about them. They are wary. They move differently, they talk less. They keep their weapons clean and ready. They wear their kit. There's an obvious lack of complacency about them. In battle-hardened troops there is an edge and also a caution. They don't just get up and do things; they look around first. They learn tricks. They go around walls rather than straight through doors. They know when to ask others to solve problems for them, so instead of just charging over the top, they'll ask for artillery or for bombs to be dropped from an airplane. It's an understanding that a soldier is taught in training yet doesn't really appreciate until he's been through an inoculation period. That's true at every rank.
>
> DAVID RICHARDS

David also worried that there weren't enough of us.

> I knew the Canadian army was small and, despite Rick Hillier's enthusiasm and the professionalism and determination out there, the fact is, they really had only a battalion-plus. A battalion on average is about 800 soldiers. The same as the British had in Helmand at that time. But the British had a bigger army to draw on. It was inevitable that we would have to draw on them at some stage because it was just too big for one battalion.
>
> DAVID RICHARDS

In fact, the Americans also had too few troops, especially in the south, which was why things were going wrong in Kandahar and Helmand. With Iraq unravelling, they simply couldn't put enough troops on task, which is why Bush and his Secretary of Defense Donald Rumsfeld were leaning on NATO to take over. Yet despite their need for NATO, the Americans' doubts about NATO's readiness were widely whispered. The Taliban in particular perked up at the news. They started to occupy what in military terms are called prime military positions in the Panjwayi Valley region. These included defensible locales with marijuana and poppy fields, high hedges, orchards, vineyards, irrigation ditches, a network of dried riverbeds called *wadis*, and a cluster of villages to the north of the Arghandab River, which formed a natural boundary virtually impossible for an attacker to cross without being repelled. Highway 1, the critical stretch of highway that was once a southern leg of the Silk Road, passed right through their territory. At any time they could foray out onto the road and destroy whatever was using it at the time.

The Taliban was in force in Panjwayi. Rather than attack from their positions, they simply defended their strongholds and warned the locals that big things were coming. Their growing presence cast a pall over the whole of Kandahar Province. In military terms, they were psychologically and physically dominating the terrain.

> People in Kabul began to say, "We can't let this keep going on, the Taliban is cocking up procedure by NATO in its first month." I started to get very interested in it. I met with David Fraser who had come to the same conclusion at the same time. We agreed that the Canadians would have to occupy this ground for two reasons: first, to defeat the Taliban at the beginning of our period in command; and second, more importantly in many respects, to show NATO countries, Afghans and Americans alike, that NATO could fight and win battles just as well as the Americans—indeed better. That was our aim. The problem was that, during August,

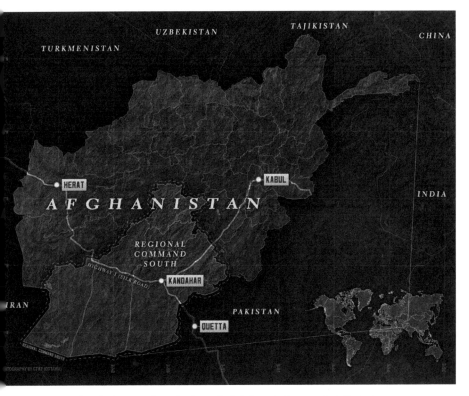

Afghanistan has been a trading nation forever. Until airplanes, trade was conducted by land or sea, and no land route has been more valuable than a series of roads, paths and passes known as the Silk Road. Already established in the second century BCE, these corridors became the chief routes for Chinese exports of high-value spices and textiles (thus the name), and they were policed and protected across vast stretches, with the Great Wall of China as the easternmost security segment. One of the main routes through India to the Mediterranean markets was the long stretch of the Silk Road that passed through Quetta in present-day Pakistan, up through Kandahar and Herat in Afghanistan, then west through the Persian Empire and on to Baghdad in Iraq. The 575-kilometre segment from Kandahar to Herat is now a paved motorway that goes by the somewhat less-romantic name of Highway 1. No matter its name, it's still the main trade route for goods out of and into Kandahar. Anyone who controls Highway 1 controls the Afghan economy. One of the aims of Operation Medusa was to prevent the Taliban from doing precisely that.

the Taliban developed a very strong defensive position and we had too few troops by military doctrinal standards—and other respects—to do the job easily, so we had to come up with a plan that reflected that.

DAVID RICHARDS

And so Medusa was born.

CHAPTER 6

SHAKE

Being a tactical guy my whole life, the easiest thing to do is bitch about staff and brigade. Then I got to Kandahar and saw the amount of work those staff officers do. Blew me away.

MOTHER

A meeting of deputy ministers took place in Ottawa on Thursday, August 7, 2006. Ward Elcock was deputy defence minster at the time. He had been in the post two full years by then and knew exactly what he was doing. Ward was a close ally of Rick Hillier and an active supporter of our efforts in Afghanistan. He, like Rick, was concerned that the pressure on the defence contingent was extreme and that other departments weren't pulling their weight. Canada's theoretical whole-of-government strategy was not materializing. Everyone talked about a three-pronged approach of defence, diplomacy and development, but defence was taking the brunt. Some Canadian diplomats were at work, mostly in the capital city of Kabul as one would expect, but the development piece was missing entirely. The Canadian International Development Agency (CIDA) was struggling with the Afghan situation. At the time it was operating primarily as a funding agency. They funnelled money to NGOs and campaigns around the world according to the priorities of the day back in Ottawa.

By then, Christina Green was our development advisor, and the only CIDA rep on the ground in RC South. Christina reported to CIDA authorities living in the relative comfort of Kabul—bureaucrats who just didn't get it. Most lacked the situational awareness needed to be able to deal with the complexities on the ground. As a group they had to evolve their methodology so they could help Afghans more directly. They had no local intelligence. No ground truth. They didn't know and couldn't know how the money they doled out was being used. An article by the Canadian Press in 2008 summed it up:

> Canada's approach is failing. Millions of dollars are eaten up by corruption and mismanagement, and even successful programs do not seem to have a long-term impact, according to govern-ment documents, non-governmental organizations and a former aid official. Nipa Banerjee said 50 per cent of the $300 million allocated during her three years as head of aid in Afghanistan for the Canadian International Development Agency brought little or no results. "Fifty per cent had impact and the other 50 didn't," said Banerjee, who ran CIDA's office in Kabul from 2003 to 2006 and now lectures at the University of Ottawa. "The 50 per cent that didn't were not in the social and economic sectors, but they were in the security sector, justice sector, the police—which have been failures." Banerjee's estimates are mirrored in a recent review of CIDA programs, released in the fall of 2007. Twelve of 27 projects CIDA had underway between 2004 and 2007 were reviewed in detail by independent professionals. Half of them were described as having "significantly improved people's lives," but the remainder were judged as mixed successes, mostly as a result of corruption and a dearth of skilled, knowledgeable people to carry out programs and keep track of spending.
>
> AS REPORTED BY THE EMBASSY OF AFGHANISTAN IN CANADA IN
> AFGHAN NEWS 01/31/2008—BULLETIN #1915

That kind of feckless programming wasn't helping us in Kandahar. We needed to prove to people on a daily basis that our commitment to their security, stability and prosperity was real. We needed more than chequebook diplomacy. We needed cash to hand out when the moment was right, which is precisely how the Americans had done it. Their lieutenants had access to ready money. When they talked to elders in villages about the pressing needs, they had the authority to hand over cash on the spot for pumps, buildings, school supplies . . . for anything that would help people get on with their lives in this chaotic and dangerous environment. When NATO took over and Canada was in charge of RC South, we had almost nothing to offer. It was more than embarrassing; it was a failure of strategy that played right into the hands of the Taliban. We proved over and over that we were lying about being there for the long haul.

We needed to shake someone.

So back in Ottawa at that meeting of deputy ministers on August 7, CIDA was struggling to adapt to the new reality on the ground. We all hoped that development activities would speed up, and in the short term they did. Our provincial reconstruction teams began all kinds of projects in Nimroz, Helmand, Kandahar, Zabul and Uruzgan (nothing in Daikundi), but never enough to convince the locals that we had their backs. The mood at that meeting in Ottawa reflected an awakening recognition in government that something had to be done to take the pressure off the military in Afghanistan. Things did begin to change. We saw more active diplomacy between Ottawa and Kabul, increased (albeit temporary) development assistance out of CIDA, faster provision of vehicles, equipment, ammunition and supplies to Kandahar, and stronger efforts to wring more support out of NATO itself.

CHAPTER 7

LEARN

Other than my wife, the thing I missed the most was grabbing gears on my Harley, having my face in the wind, and letting all the bullshit flow. That's why I brought my Harley mirrors with me and mounted them on my turret.

MOTHER

A s we operated in theatre, we were astonished daily by our own ignorance. Coming out of the most intensive training to which Canadian soldiers had ever been subjected in peacetime, many of us had assumed we were prepared. This wasn't an arrogant assumption. We had digested all the doctrinal manuals and studied enemy tactics and battlefield manoeuvres at length. We had been given unlimited staff and materiel with which to build pre-deployment exercises that stretched us in every imaginable way. We had challenged ourselves with team-testing command-post scenarios, subjected ourselves to high-intensity battle simulations and conducted full-on, live-fire exercises. We had refined our communications protocols and decision-making models using real-time feeds from theatre, interacting with active units already in Afghanistan. The list went on and on and on. We had never been this well trained for anything.

But we were still nowhere near ready.

With national and international political pressures, wildly accelerated timelines and daily risk to life and limb, the world we entered was its own mad reality. Nothing could prepare us for the number, range and intensity of operations we had to undertake but those operations themselves.

The first few months on the ground after arriving in February were fast. We installed our brigade, composed (as Ben Freakley had worried about) of soldiers still inexperienced in the combination of combat operations and national reconstruction we had taken on. The Americans we relieved were combat veterans with many tours in Afghanistan and Iraq under their belts. They had grown up in the United States military, a brilliantly engineered, hard-driving and fiercely competitive system that produces arguably the world's most effective warriors. Those were big shoes to fill.

It might be helpful here to review some terminology. Mission-focused brigades like ours in RC South are supported by dedicated on-site headquarters staff, which in our case we had stationed at the Kandahar Airfield. That brigade relies for its effect on units of trained military personnel who join the mission (or, as we say, arrive in theatre) as part of a task force created for the mission at hand. Those personnel come from home units in Canada, typically of 500 to 700 soldiers each, known as either battalions or regiments. Both these terms refer to groups of the same size. The difference is only that infantry units and service support units use the term "battalion," while armoured, engineer and artillery units use the term "regiment." In Canada, these battalions and regiments recruit, train and manage military personnel but never deploy on overseas missions in their existing configurations. When it's time for operations, they assign their personnel to a larger force which, depending on the need, may be configured as its own distinct battalion, a task force (such as Task Force Orion which went to Afghanistan in early 2006 and Task Force 3-06 which replaced them in August of that year), a brigade, division or even an army. But no matter the size, each of these operational formations will be tailor-made for its mission with personnel and equipment suited to the specific nature of the environment and the specific threat expected within it.

To understand the scale of an operation, it's useful to know that a brigade normally has a mix of three infantry battalions, one armoured regiment, one engineer regiment, one service battalion, an artillery regiment and other support units, together numbering some 4,000–5,000 troops. A division is a larger unit still, with 10,000 or even 20,000 soldiers under its command.

Canada has long been a battalion-centric army, and as such has been focused on giving battalion commanders the training and operational experience they need to be effective. But Canadian command of brigade-level operations in combat has been rare since the 1940s. All that changed when we agreed to run RC South. While battalions such as those commanded in Afghanistan by Ian Hope and Omer Lavoie would have their own steep learning curves, we at the brigade level would have a hell of a time figuring out how to manage multiple battalions, international partners, aviation, materiel, medical care, reporting up multiple chains of command, and the gnarly politics of a coalition operating in an area of one million square kilometres. The Americans, who have had continual experience at all levels, found operations in Afghanistan well within the level of their skill and experience. Not us. We had a lot to learn.

While we couldn't appreciate it at the time, we were fortunate to begin our tour with a number of low-intensity missions. These built over time in both tempo and complexity, which allowed us to work out the kinks and improve our speed of response. As we rose to the operational tempo required to build a nation while fighting a counter-insurgency, we also had to accommodate the arrival in spring of the British into Helmand and the Dutch into Uruzgan, two vital provinces within RC South. That involved complex international logistics undertaken while engaging the enemy.

As the British built a support base in the spring of 2006 to house their 3rd Battalion, Parachute Regiment (3 PARA) in Helmand and the Dutch established themselves in Uruzgan, it fell to the Canadians to keep the Taliban fully occupied in those two provinces as well as Kandahar. This job was taken on by Lieutenant Colonel Ian Hope and

I have known Ian Hope for many years. I was Ian's battalion commander in the 2nd Battalion PPCLI, and we served in Bosnia when he was a company commander. He has worked for me as a staff officer and his intellect is well known. Ian is a charismatic and passionate officer who throws himself into whatever he does. He is single-minded and a hard charger. Ian had a great roster of non-commissioned members and officers who commanded outstanding troops. Ian took personal interest in every mission outside the wire, and was there in front all the time. 1 PPCLI did a great job taking over from the American Task Force Gun Devil. During Ian's six months in theatre, he led his unit through countless operations and distinguished himself and his unit in fights in Sangin, Garmsir and throughout Kandahar. I flew home to Edmonton following his tour to conduct his change of command parade. All who attended had great and justifiable respect for everything his unit had accomplished.

his Task Force Orion. From the get-go, their aim was to move around the region looking for Taliban nests to prod.

Ian was just the guy to take on the task. He was bright and confident. He related well to his soldiers, in part because he had served in the ranks himself before taking his commission. An independent thinker with strong, sometimes aggressive opinions, Ian was also a good communicator who kept everyone around him informed. He was tough to manage but manageable. As commanding officer of the Canadian army's 1st Battalion, Princess Patricia's Canadian Light Infantry (1 PPCLI) in 2005, he had been the obvious choice to lead Task Force Orion, which then spent the first part of its six-month tour in Afghanistan travelling throughout RC South to fight the Taliban. With Task Force Orion on the job, our partners had the time to settle in and the provincial reconstruction teams time to bolster economic development.

With Task Force Orion busy in the field and my brigade headquarters fully engaged with RC South, our education began in earnest in February 2006. Not a day went by from then till August without a lesson learned. But four incidents in particular taught us about the Taliban—and about ourselves—in ways that would prove instrumental during Operation Medusa.

Our first big test came during the brigade-level Operation Grant's Return in Zabul Province in June. RC South moved the bulk of the American 2nd Battalion, 4th Infantry Regiment into the northern reaches of Zabul Province to re-establish government authority along a great swath of Taliban-controlled territory. Canadians hadn't been involved in an operation of this scope since the Korean War, and managing the vast number of assets in play alone was a daunting prospect. Detailed planning was critical to make sure logistics, manoeuvre and intelligence were all coordinated. Doing that competently while learning on the job was a challenge. This was especially true at the brigade level, given the number and variety of assets under our control, and it required that we master the art of complex operations across all three lines of operation: governance, defence and development.

The second occurred in Helmand that same month. Just as the United Kingdom's 3 PARA was due to arrive in the province, a *kandak* (battalion) of the Afghan National Army (ANA) was ambushed coming out of the village of Kajaki on the eastern banks of the Helmand River. Kajaki was the site of a hydroelectric power dam with great economic and strategic importance to the region. The attack on the ANA battalion by the Taliban highlighted the complexity of activity in the region and the disparate chains of command in Afghanistan. The ANA neither reported nor coordinated their activities with us. Even their embedded American trainers reported to a different authority. They didn't communicate with us at all. Similarly, the U.S. special forces operated on different systems, answering to a separate chain of command. And yet we operated in the same space, so trying to help our soldiers when they were in contact with the enemy was a messy business.

After a vicious, day-long firefight, the battered Afghan soldiers made it to Forward Operating Base Wolf (later called FOB Robinson). We had decided to send a Canadian platoon from our regional reserve to reinforce the embattled Afghan soldiers, who were seriously fatigued after their ordeal. But things got worse. A tired American soldier, muddled in the chaos of battle, killed one Canadian and one American soldier and injured many others. To stabilize the situation ahead of the arrival of the British into Helmand, I ordered Major Bill Fletcher and a platoon from Charlie Company into Sangin, the notorious hub of the opium trade about 30 kilometres downriver from Kajaki. The five-day action we had anticipated turned into weeks of intermittent fighting, with the Taliban once again taking control of this lucrative drug-production centre.

It was essential to avoid 3 PARA having to fight their way into theatre, so we decided to raise the stakes. Under Operation Mountain Thrust (our first time in the box as the divisional main effort) Ben Freakley gave us the 2nd Battalion, 87th Infantry Regiment (2-87), a combat-experienced task force from RC East. Supported by aviation, they would form up with Ian Hope's 1 PPCLI, the incoming British 3 PARA, units of the Afghan ANA and other NATO forces to re-establish Afghan governance in Helmand Province. The immediate challenge was to disrupt the enemy before, ultimately, taking Sangin back from the Taliban. This effort was preceded by sizeable special forces operations in northern Helmand and adjacent areas in Uruzgan, after which the formation was handed over to me. Our job was to plan for and execute an attack on Sangin on July 16, which we were able to do with 2-87, 1 PPCLI, 3 PARA, Afghan and Estonian forces — more than 2,500 troops in all. They pressed into the town from three different directions, eventually wresting the district centre from the enemy, then cordoning off and clearing the Taliban compounds at key locations in the town.

The retaking of Sangin was the first brigade attack conducted under Canadian command since the Second World War. Our planning was exhaustive, our rehearsals comprehensive — yet despite our efforts, our execution was less than perfect. Inexperience on the part of some coalition partners resulted in critical missteps in timing. Chief among them, the British paratroopers from 3 PARA arrived a full 45 minutes after the time set for the three-pronged strike. This was further aggravated by the interference of their national contingent commander, Brigadier Ed Butler.

> That totally disrupted the synchronization of joint fires and intelligence collection. The timeline was completely disrupted, and not by the enemy but by the coalition arrangements. And they're fighting with different equipment, different doctrine and those caveats that affect what people will really do. You have some leaders who are committed to what they need to do and many leaders who are not.
>
> BEN FREAKLEY

Because we failed to execute as a single force with overwhelming pressure, we allowed many of the enemy to slip away even as we were retaking the town. Granted, governmental authority had been re-established, no coalition casualties had been incurred, and our formation had had a good workout that day, so in many ways the operation had been a success. Yet our inexperience had cost us. We had in no way achieved all our intended effects. We had to get better.

And we did. Springing from our experiences at the start of the mission and in battles such as Sangin, we learned enough to be able to launch short-notice operations with better effect, so the next big lesson was positive. I will never forget my radio communication with Ian Hope right after securing Sangin. I told him that before returning to Kandahar he had to take his troops south down the Helmand River to rout the Taliban out of a town called Garmsir. He instantly committed. I asked if he had the men, equipment and ammunition to do the job. He assured me he did. I asked if he had any questions. He said, "Just one. Where the hell is Garmsir?"

Understandable. At the time, we hardly knew these small towns and villages. Many were simply too small to be on any of our charts. To guide Ian onto target, I drew a map of the Helmand River, putting an X where I thought Garmsir was. In a notable fusion of low tech and high tech, I then dispatched that hand-drawn chart to him by helicopter with the advice, "Head toward this spot until they fire at you. Then you'll know you've found Garmsir." Ably supported by a talented logistics team under Lieutenant Colonel John Conrad, Ian Hope and his Patricias deployed swiftly and smartly to the south. When they met the enemy, they acted decisively. After fierce fighting they captured the two towns of Garmsir and Nawa. Their success illustrated just how far we had come.

Our tempo was like nothing we could have imagined before. At the brigade level, our average daily activity was nineteen significant activities (SIGACTS), which typically included repelling six rocket-propelled grenade (RPG) attacks, two mortar attacks, five small-arms attacks, one sniper attack and one improvised explosive device (IED) attack, necessitating at least four medevacs. Brutal.

But advancement along the learning curve was not ours alone; the Taliban were educating themselves at the same rate. Whenever we employed a novel and successful tactic, they would evaluate the factors underlying their defeat and evolve. Such is the progress of armed conflict. We saw this during an incident I offer as my fourth example. It occurred on August 3, when Ian Hope attacked into Panjwayi on his way back to Kandahar from one of his many excursions into Taliban-dominated terrain. Determined to harass the enemy one more time, he swung up a roadway in Pashmul, just north of the Arghandab River, to an American-built white schoolhouse complex. One of his lead vehicles hit an IED and, when that happened, the Taliban, who had been waiting undercover, rose and fired on the stranded vehicle and those behind it. In the ensuing fierce firefight, many were wounded, while Sergeant Vaughan Ingram, Corporals Christopher Reid and Bryce Keller, and Private Kevin Dallaire were killed in action. It was at this point we understood we'd seen something new. Never before had we encountered an IED incident covered by fire. The Taliban had changed their behaviour, and that day we learned a cruel lesson on just how fluid operations and conditions were going to be in Afghanistan.

By then Ian and his troops were all experienced and battle-hardened. They had conducted themselves exceptionally throughout their tour — but paradoxically, through their persistent and deliberate irritation, had forced the Taliban to pick up their game. August 3 had been a bloody day for all, and it was to be the opening salvo in the build-up to Operation Medusa.

CHAPTER 8

THINK

We'd be heading out, and I'd say to the Boss, "We can't go because you don't have your helmet on. Until you do, we're not leaving." He'd have a little tantrum, put it on, then we'd go.

MOTHER

Something had changed on August 3 and we all knew it, but for a long time we couldn't figure it out. Ian Hope had hit the hornet's nest at the white schoolhouse. After charging around the region for six full months, he had better insight than anyone about what was going on. He was the first to realize that things had changed and that it was bad. The Taliban had come to the conclusion that they could finish us off.

Insurgents are rebels fighting against either a government or an invading force. Typically they use hit-and-run techniques, because they don't have the strength or firepower to conduct an all-out battle using conventional tactics. Their approach is to disrupt, confuse and frustrate their foe rather than destroy it. Military doctrine holds that when insurgents move from guerrilla to conventional tactics, it's an indication that they have gained confidence in their ability to resolve the campaign quickly in their favour. That's what was going on here, but no one was talking to us about it. We were being kept in the dark. I was dealing with the Asadullah Khalid, Governor of Kandahar Province, on a daily basis, and yet he hadn't confided in me. The Taliban was moving into his region to kill us all and then lay siege to his own city, and he was just talking about how long it takes to get grapes to market.

It sank in slowly: *they think they can beat us.* As our intel came together day by day, we formed a clearer picture of where they were and what they were up to. Now it was up to us to decide what to do in response.

I had to figure out how to fight a force digging in for a conventional battle. We hadn't been trained or deployed for anything this big. That was not our mission. Ours was counter-insurgency—and nation-building within a counter-insurgency. We just weren't manned, equipped or armed to do a major assault. But there we were. No use complaining. Better just do something about it.

This is how the rough planning of Operation Medusa started. I took the time to think. Running through my head were things like this: *I just know they want to give me the biggest, blackest, bloodiest eye they can. They want to kill lots of us, and they're now confident they can do a ton of damage.*

I started reassessing how many casualties we were going to suffer, musing that the Taliban probably had already done their own assessment. I couldn't afford many casualties. Beyond the obvious waste of young Canadian lives, it would be unacceptable back home. And if I lost the battle, which the Taliban fully expected, they would achieve all their aims. I looked at disposition charts that showed where they were and realized if I went in and attacked first from either the east or the north, I'd be attacking them in their positions of greatest strength. By attacking from the south instead, the Arghandab River would be both a tough obstacle and a considerable advantage. The flow rate was not high at the time, but a river crossing was always risky during an advance, and yet the river would be as much of an obstacle to the Taliban as it would be to us.

The Arghandab would give us some distance. We could stand off and observe first, then fire as required with our LAV (light armoured vehicle) cannons and artillery, and drop ordnance with air support. We could also use our surveillance technology to our advantage. We'd know where they were, and they sure as hell wouldn't be moving fast or far once this thing began. An approach from the south would be difficult, but less risky than one from another direction.

My second consideration was the intensity of the upcoming battle. I saw it this way: *Against five hundred bad guys led by their top ten commanders, this is going to be a hard fight with a lot of killing. I have to minimize the amount of killing of my own soldiers.*

Avoiding deaths was not only mandatory—in today's political climate there are deep ramifications any time our soldiers fall. I needed to keep casualties to a minimum, yet I had to risk soldiers' lives to get this thing done. So how would I fight this? I could go the conventional way and just storm in and shoot my way through each objective in turn, but I didn't have the combat forces I needed to do that, and I knew I wasn't going to get more any time soon. I thought, *My hands are tied, my feet are tied, and I'm gagged and blindfolded. How do I beat them?*

Then I remembered that I had seen this exact scenario before, not in my own career but in Les Grau's history of the British and Russian campaigns in Afghanistan. In *The Other Side of the Mountain*, Grau observed that attacking forces always rely on conventional tactics when they fight Afghans on their own turf, and every time they lose. When the Brits tried it in 1839, they sent in nearly 20,000 soldiers. They fought a conventional war while the Afghans fought a guerrilla war. Basically, the Afghans acted like insurgents in their own country. Never once did they mass for an attack. Instead they used small raiding parties, ambushes in mountain passes, quick attacks on city streets. The Afghan fighters blended in with their own population. No uniforms. The Brits could never tell who was the enemy until a second or two before they were slaughtered. Three years later, there was only one British soldier left alive. Twenty thousand guys went in and only one came out. No fucking way I was going to do that.

I'm not going to win by rolling in and fighting this guy, I reasoned. *I have to find another way. I'm going to go slow. He's wearing the watch but we've got the time. I'm going to stand off. I'm going to observe. I'm going to listen in. I'm going to fly over and get a full surveillance picture. I'm going to use psychological ops. I'm going to move my own guys around, confuse him, make him wonder where we are and what we're up* to. *I'm just going to take my time, and then every time he sticks his head up, I'm going to whack it off.*

The Taliban was adopting a conventional defensive position, and I would refuse to take the expected conventional offensive position. I decided we would become the insurgents. I thought, *He's turned out to be like me so I'm going to become him. I'll attack him, but I'll do it in an unconventional way. I'm going to play whack-a-mole.* And that's what I told the guys: "I got it. We're reversing our roles. Let's go plan it out."

CHAPTER 9

STUDY

Americans criticized the LAV III as not being good on the terrain in Afghanistan. Correct me if I'm wrong, but I think a lot of that comes down to driver skill. Greg Moon could put a LAV through that doorway over there without ever leaving a scratch.

MOTHER

We never set out to plan a glorious victory with Operation Medusa. Subsequent criticisms have taken pains to imply that there was no enduring victory and that therefore Operation Medusa has been assigned more credit than it deserves. But in truth we set out with a humble objective: not to lose.

Here's why. By winning in Panjwayi, the Taliban could set up a safe haven in a district from which they could launch operations to isolate Kandahar. And this isolation would have a deep impact. The end state they imagined was the removal of all government and ISAF control in Zhari, Panjwayi and Kandahar City. It would mean the successful achievement of their stated objective, which was to destabilize the government of Afghanistan.

A loss for us would bolster Taliban resolve immeasurably. It would make it possible for them to increase their recruiting and their fundraising. They would then be able to solidify their links back to Pakistan, with an inevitable increase in the flow of weapons, ammunition and drugs across national borders, along the myriad ratlines that served as feeder routes for the whole area—and, ultimately, in broad daylight along a Taliban-controlled Highway 1. And the Kandahar Afghan Development Zone (ADZ), one of the key concepts proposed in the General Richards–approved ISAF plan, would never happen — with all its projects to rebuild schools, dig irrigation canals and repair roadways in the many communities that needed them simply abandoned. So the day after Ian Hope's group stumbled into an ambush at the white schoolhouse on August 3, we began to plan the large-scale, complex kinetic action that would become Operation Medusa.

The Taliban had probably also figured out that a resounding defeat of ISAF forces would be met with horror by the home populations of participating NATO nations, whose governments would then likely question their overseas commitments amid the public outcry. And they were right. We Canadians knew that after reporting a major loss of Canadian lives in Afghanistan, Harper's minority government would come under deafening criticism from opposition parties smelling an opportunity. The Brits knew that the same was true of their own government, which had already demonstrated its lack of resolve by sending troops into Helmand in such a reduced state that they couldn't operate effectively. They moved out in day patrols only, unable to staff and supply a single forward operating base even if they wanted to. When British troops moved by vehicle, it was often in unarmoured Land Rovers, some of which didn't even have doors.

The fall of Kandahar would also send waves of distrust through the fledgling government in Kabul, proving to the population that it had neither the brains nor the brawn to deal with the Taliban as promised. As such, we judged the most dangerous outcome to be the establishment by the Taliban of a permanent operating base in the districts of Panjwayi and Zhari, likely using the market town of Bazar-e-Panjwayi. From such a hub they could launch a series of attacks to block the routes into Kandahar City for as long as they wanted.

We knew the insurgents' likely course of action. They would continue to use attacks in the vicinity of Pashmul to draw the ISAF and Afghan National Security Forces (ANSF) into Taliban-prepared defensive positions. Our soldiers would then have to fight on foot, and could be either ambushed from thick cover or crippled by IEDs as they advanced over terrain intimately known by the enemy.

From the outset, we began weighing up our chances of success. We had many advantages: We knew their defensive positions. We knew their staging areas. We could see them from the air and listen in on their mobile phone conversations, as unencrypted cell phones were their chief means of communication.

But while we all knew that failure was not an option for us, failure was a very real prospect. The Taliban had many distinct advantages over our own forces. First, they were seasoned soldiers with high morale on a campaign with deep spiritual significance to them. They all spoke the local language, knew the local customs and recognized all the local people on sight, many of whom they had already intimidated by violence into doing their bidding.

> The Taliban are not an insignificant force. They are sometimes portrayed by the media and others as a ragtag, spontaneous group of a few people who fight. That's really a poor generalization of a very competent political, military, economic and social entity. Yes, the tribes will themselves fight, but they will also outsource violence to others. Historically, the Mujahideen were joined by foreign fighters—Chechens, Saudi Arabians and others—who came to fight as part of the Mujahideen against the Russians. That established a tradition of paying for security. One of the tactics of the Mujahideen, and now of the Taliban, was to overrun a district station, police station or government station and then say to the population, "See? They can't secure you. The Russians can't secure you. Those loyal to the Russians can't secure you. We the Mujahideen have taken over this area. We'll secure you." So there is psychological pressure to reconsider who can provide security whenever these district police stations are overrun.
>
> BEN FREAKLEY

The Taliban also knew every millimetre of the local terrain, had made smart choices about where to cache weapons and ammunitions, and had stored enough food to last through a sustained action. This capability for tactical resupply gave them extraordinary staying power.

They had effective small-unit tactics (arguably more seasoned than most of our own, given the lack of combat experience of our only recently arrived troops). They worked and fought together in tight sections of four to ten men. They had an ability to concentrate forces strategically against any attacking force to maximum effect, as they had proved handsomely to the Soviets. Most of their senior commanders had first bloodied themselves in those battles against the Russians.

Their knowledge of their enemy was high: for one thing, they knew our tactics, having seen them unfold in as many as twenty-five incidents per day since we arrived in February. They had studied how we moved, when and why we dismounted, and how we regrouped and withdrew. They had extensive early-warning systems, all of them human—from cooperative villagers and urban contacts in Kandahar to spies within the ANSF, and particularly from within the police who were notoriously corrupt. They had deeply entrenched information operations between Panjwayi and Pakistan, the abetting nation in which they carried out their fundraising, recruiting and training.

Finally, they were hard to find. They did not wear uniforms and, with their local stashes of weapons and ammunition, could move unencumbered until coming to an assembly area where they could pick up everything they needed. They knew the ground. They moved among the people. In most cases, they *were* the people.

They were also aided greatly by the terrain. We could tell that just by looking in. On the south side of the Arghandab River stands a small mountain known as M'sūm Ghar. *Ghar* is the Pashto word for "mount," as in Mount Olympus in Greece or Mount Rushmore in South Dakota. M'sūm Ghar lies just south of Bazar-e-Panjwayi, on the road from Kandahar. The view from the mountain is spectacular—clear

across the Arghandab River to a rolling expanse of lush fields inter-
rupted by dozens of ancient villages (hamlets really), farmers' houses,
storage sheds, and grape-drying huts of clay that are four feet thick in
places. Fed by water from the river, this area is one of the most fertile
in the region.

Poppy fields are common further from the river at the outer
edges of the district, while vineyards are everywhere, filled with earth-
trellised clumps of fruit that produce nine-tenths of Afghanistan's
grapes for export. Once gathered, the grapes are moved to narrow
drying houses called *kishmish khana*. These huts are also armoured
bunkers. With deep walls pierced by ventilation slits, they're like
Martello towers. The Taliban routinely use them as storehouses for
weapons and munitions, control centres and, during actual firefights,
bomb shelters. A 25mm shell fired from the turret of a LAV III will
bounce right off the walls. Even with solid-rocket propulsion, an
M72 light anti-tank round fired at the same wall will produce plenty
of rubble but few actual holes.

Of the ordnance we had at our disposal, the only effective offence
against *kishmish khana* came from our 155mm howitzers and bombs
dropped from aircraft. Bombs were effective when on target, but only
because the damage to the building was total. In such cases, collateral
damage was a constant risk. The enemy inside could be killed with
one bomb blast, but the long-term effect on the community might be
severe. The Taliban knew this: they dug into these structures in force,
daring us to come and get them just as they had dared the Soviets to
do. A telling fact is that, despite having 115,000 Soviet troops in the
country at any one time who busily slaughtered between 75,000 and
90,000 Mujahideen fighters, no Soviet flag ever flew over a single
Panjwayi village. We were well aware of that as the launch date for
Operation Medusa drew closer.

The terrain, therefore, clearly favoured the defender. While easy
enough to see through and over, earth-trellised vineyards were perilous
to cross. With every footfall we risked triggering an IED. And marijuana

M'sūm Ghar, at the top of this photo, is the site where in August Mike Wright had his first engagement against a sizeable Taliban force. M'sūm Ghar would become very familiar to 1 RCR as they staged out of there, attacking across the Arghandab River (to the left) into Objective Rugby. Immediately to the southwest (bottom of the picture) lay Sperwan Ghar, the site of some of the fiercest fighting during Operation Medusa. It never ceased to amaze any of us how areas like this, with little to no cover, could be areas of tremendous strategic importance to the Taliban. Sperwan was the home to a Taliban training site, which was a complete surprise to everyone. It might account for why Mike Wright had encountered a large enemy force nearby, and it was certainly the reason that Task Force 31 had to fight intensely to capture it. It took us days to rout the old Soviet outpost from the Taliban, with tremendous loss of life on their side as they countered our attacks with fighters from across the Arghandab River in Siah Choy. The terrain in this picture will be forever burned into the memories of those who fought there. This was the Taliban's key location and they fought dearly for it. TF 31 was later honoured by Canada's Governor General with the Commander-in-Chief Unit Commendation for incredible accomplishment in the face of the enemy.

Afghanistan is a beautiful country. The mountains and deserts and the forests in the north are breathtaking. I understand why this was a country that attracted tourists in happier times. During our forays into the countryside, we came across hundreds if not thousands of poppy fields like this. Poppy is considered by Afghans much as our own farmers consider corn or wheat; it is a cash crop, and the yield off a field like this will support a family for most of the year. Our challenge was twofold: garner the support of the locals who grew crops like this and distance ourselves from those intent on destroying these crops. Inevitably, our troops would be there when a field was being destroyed and therefore we would be associated with destroying the livelihood of some local. We wrote a letter to the authorities suggesting farm subsidies for crops other than poppy. It was never looked at in any seriousness. Alas, this complication made our job of trying to build a nation and winning over the people next to impossible.

fields were their own kind of horror. Each dense forest of cannabis offered a different and forbidding microclimate. A platoon making its way through would have to navigate a dark, sticky obstacle course with temperatures of 50 degrees Celsius and 99 per cent humidity. These steam baths were everywhere.

While the terrain might have been an advantage to the Taliban, they had many notable weaknesses we intended to exploit. First, they were tied to the very terrain they knew so well. They had no air support for transport, surveillance, resupply or evacuation. They arrived in or near Panjwayi in their fleets of Toyota Hilux pickup trucks, but once in theatre they had to go almost everywhere on foot. While this made them harder to find (vehicles being easier to spot), it made them slow to redeploy. And their limited operational mobility made them easy to pursue once they had abandoned their defences. It also meant they had no medical capability beyond first-line treatment. If a seriously wounded fighter could not be treated on site, his likelihood of recovery was minimal.

Over and over we had witnessed the Taliban's inability to sustain a firefight. We knew—and they had experienced—that after thirty minutes in any engagement they would suffer severely. After that could I guarantee to have attack helicopters, fast air (aircraft such as A-10 Warthogs that could move in quickly) and bombers on hand— whatever it would take to strengthen our response and win the engagement. Whenever troops come into contract with the enemy, an event we call *troops in contact* or TIC, we move in to support them. While it might take us half an hour to get to the party, we would then have the ability to unleash hell. That half-hour window became a focal point for us. I told each of my commanders that in any engagement, the first thirty minutes was his to fight. From brigade headquarters we would ensure that everyone had artillery and medevac in that period, but our guys on the ground would have to fight the furious opening act on their own. The Taliban got to know this, and typically disappeared after thirty minutes of any fight to avoid being pounded.

Elements of resupply posed another limitation to the Taliban. Depending on the location and event, they were restricted to any supplies of weapons and ammunitions they had cached in advance. Some IED components such as blasting caps were difficult for them to procure. Medical treatment and supplies were another issue. Before any planned combat, doctors who were either sympathetic to or coerced by the Taliban would come in and create pop-up clinics and dispensaries, so we made a point of looking for them. We learned that even just the sight of someone new working in a pharmacy was a good indication of a forthcoming action. We routinely intercepted and dismantled their medical supply chains to make it harder for them to treat and evacuate their wounded. This then forced them to use local hospitals. Whenever random farmers began showing up at Kandahar's Allama Rishad or Mirwais Nika hospitals—or even the Kandahar University Faculty of Medicine—with severe, traumatic injuries, we knew that the Taliban's front-line medical services had crumpled. Our interventions were being effective.

Their command structure was also a liability. At least until the time of Operation Medusa, the Taliban fought with a command-centric organization in which a small handful of seasoned leaders planned, monitored and directed every aspect of operations in the field. Our own command structure used a multi-level chain of authority, from the brigade commander to the battalion commander to his company commanders to their platoon commanders, and eventually to section commanders who each directed ten or so men and women. In the case of the Taliban, there were usually fewer than three links in that chain, and often just two. Taliban fighters had no local authority. They would wait to be told from on high what to do. We knew that if we could knock out the small number of senior commanders in any area, we could effectively freeze their decision-making ability.

Communication was perhaps the Taliban's most exploitable weakness. While we worked on multiple frequencies with many layers of encryption, they used only VHF and GSM for cell phone, handheld radio and satellite phone comms, none of which were secure. We used their transmissions to vector in on where they were. We listened in all the time, and sometimes even phoned one of them up directly to tell him what we wanted him to hear.

Lastly, they had limited night vision. Night vision goggles are expensive. Whether monocular or binocular, they require image intensifier tubes milled to rigid tolerances. Tough to come by. Almost everything we owned had night-vision capability, from Predator drones to rifle sights. We could see anything the Taliban got up to, even on the darkest nights. They had no such ability, which forced them to attack only in the light. By evening civil twilight, they were quiet.

Given the strengths and weaknesses of the Taliban, our planning established six discrete categories of high-value targets we intended to hit hard early on. The first targets were their commanders, and with them the tools they used to communicate with their troops. Every senior officer is a worthy target in combat, and with the Taliban's disproportionate span of control, the loss of any one leader would leave huge numbers of fighters rudderless. By August our intel confirmed that ten or so of these senior commanders had taken up positions in Panjwayi, so we made sure their likely locations were identified as critical objectives in our battle plan.

Our second high-level targets were the factories where IEDs were made and the bomb-building teams who assembled them were trained. In the early years, the Taliban had simply repurposed Russian anti-tank mines as IEDs. Later, they perfected the art of loading explosives into used cooking-oil containers. As long as they could source blasting caps, production was fast and cheap. They had factories throughout the district—once those factories were gone, we could be sure that any road we cleared would stay that way.

Next were their indirect fire assets. These were the mortars and anti-tank rockets used to fire against remote targets. Taliban mortar teams varied in proficiency. There weren't many of them, but in 2006 most were concentrated in Helmand and Kandahar, so we had our hands full. Before Medusa, we had destroyed one crew in Kandahar, and I remember being painfully impressed by the accuracy of another such crew in Helmand (we never did get those lads). Their mortars were the 82mm Russian-made weapons left after the defeat of the Soviets in 1989.

Virtually all of the Taliban weapons and ammunition were and are of Soviet origin. The country, much like the Balkans in the 1990s, was one huge ammo depot. The Red Army left so much ordnance stashed across the country that the Taliban were never short of things to throw at us. Perversely, they had an easier time getting ammo than the Afghan police and Afghan National Army did. Small arms, mortars and anti-tank mines were all available to those willing to dig them up—and, in the event of an urgent requirement, arms merchants in Pakistan would happily fill the gap.

Rocket launchers were a unique threat. The Taliban used the Russian-made RPG-7, a shoulder-launched, rocket-propelled grenade launcher that remains the darling of insurgents and guerrillas world-wide. They fired rockets in salvoes at our passing helicopters, so when travelling by air we all kept a sharp eye on the ground for telltale smoke blasts. But even when fired from the shoulder by an expert marksman, the RPG is really only effective under 1,000 metres. So the Taliban had to bring these weapons in close to make a kill. We were often surprised, sometimes fatally, by the stealth of their rocket teams. While the threat from these weapons compelled us to designate them as high-level targets at the outset of Operation Medusa, it was really their operators we were after. Proficiency in indirect fire assets demanded a high level of training, and killing one insurgent who had that training always created more of an impact than killing several green recruits toting AK-47s. We knew that once the operators of these assets were neutralized, Taliban attack capability would be seriously degraded. So we planned to do exactly that.

Fourth on our list was the Taliban's combat service support—everything other than weapons, troops and ammo they needed to accomplish their combat missions. This included supply, maintenance, transportation, medical treatment, and all other services used to keep their fighters on the battlefield. Many of these elements were moved into the region through the Red Desert, and so I knew we had to close those routes early on. We had to stop infiltration.

> Of course you have close proximity to Pakistan, so you had people coming in from the west of Helmand into Kandahar Province. You had people coming from the south, and people even coming from the east. They could have infiltrated from the north, but Ian Hope's Princess Patricia's Canadian Light Infantry had done a lot of work there. For infiltration, the northern part of Kandahar was much more stable than the east, west or south.
>
> BEN FREAKLEY

Fifth came their intelligence, surveillance and reconnaissance capability. Most of their intel came from human sources—locals either sympathetic to or under the control of the Taliban. There were two ways to stop that flow of information. The first was to prove through consistent development activities that we were of greater value to the locals than the Taliban. (In my view, NATO failed miserably at this, and still does.) The second was to remove those sources from an area, which we intended to do in Panjwayi by dropping leaflets announcing an imminent attack. Ironically, the Taliban were themselves about to do this, by banishing civilians from the area as they dug in for the battle of the decade. Well, most civilians. They would keep enough behind to use as human shields during our air attacks.

Lastly, we had to weaken their information operations, better known as propaganda. We were not the only ones waging a campaign to win the hearts and minds of the local villagers. Every time we had a TIC with the Taliban and withdrew afterward (which was always), the insurgents would hail the event as their victory and tell lusty stories of yet another resounding NATO defeat. They couldn't drop leaflets from the air, but after dark they posted announcements in the doorways of local huts and houses. We collected these so-called night letters to learn what they were saying.

All in all, as we moved toward Operation Medusa we felt we knew the enemy well; however, that would be no guarantee of our success. The battlegrounds of history are littered with the bones of armies who knew their enemies well.

CHAPTER 10

ENGAGE

When we moved the Boss in the LAV, he just sat on an old box in the back. But we also had to take some shooters for protection, so we stripped out the main seats and added some swing seats for the guys. We also put in a coffee maker and a sandwich maker. We pimped his ride.

MOTHER

I t was standard operating procedure that when we had troops in contact, I would be informed. I would then head to the operations centre in RC South, a plywood building adjacent to Kandahar Airfield that was part of our headquarters. This nerve centre housed the main elements of the formation, including our intelligence, planning, operations and command teams. The operations room was run by our chief of operations (CHOPS), Lieutenant Colonel Tim Bishop. A seasoned artillery officer, Tim was simply immune to stress. Never have I seen another person handle pressure and complexity with the poise and confidence that Tim displayed. The only indication I ever had from him that a situation had turned bad was his asking to speak to me in my office.

The tactical operations centre (TOC) was dominated by a wall of knowledge: a broad sweep of oversized computer monitors displaying Predator feeds, live charts tracking the locations of every unit and incident, dynamic checklists that kept us on track, and a seemingly endless stream of intelligence from other sources. Beneath this array of

information stood two rows of desks at which men and women refer-
enced individual computer screens as they interacted with troops in
the field, our higher headquarters in Kabul and Canada, and the operations staff of other organizations. These were our liaison officers from
all subordinate units such as 1 RCR, our flanking formations, and aviation, medical, logistics, legal, artillery, ISR (intelligence, surveillance
and reconnaissance) and so on. We had people connected to every unit
and enabler we controlled, cooperated with or reported to. And we
needed every bit of it to maintain a high situational awareness and be
able to respond to any event.

At the back of the room were several claustrophobically small
offices, including Tim's. As CHOPS, Tim was my minute-to-minute
leader. He managed operations within the region day and night. Whenever there was an incident, he informed me immediately and, if necessary, I would come to the TOC to lead. There I had everyone I needed to
give me the right information to make informed decisions and coordinate the fight. This was also the location from which we pushed assets
to any affected "call sign" (our jargon for a unit or individual with whom
we were in contact). It was in this room that I learned about Major Mike
Wright's engagement with a sizeable Taliban force south of M'sūm
Ghar. Little did we know then that these fighters had come out of
Sperwan Ghar just a little further south, which proved the build-up of
enemy in an area other than across the river.

Mike and the company of PPCLI soldiers he commanded had been in
Afghanistan since August 4, the day after three of their fellow Patricias had
been killed in the ambush at the white schoolhouse. I had known Mike
since 1997 when I took over 2 PPCLI. Mike was a platoon commander.
I spotted him early on as someone worth nurturing. Technically competent, studious, understated and unflappable, he did everything asked
of him without fuss or fanfare.

In Afghanistan, Mike's A Company had taken responsibility for the
districts of Zhari, Panjwayi and Maywand. They had been frequently

ambushed along the main highway in the region and at Patrol Base Wilson in Zhari District. Their freedom of movement was therefore severely limited, which was frustrating as our concept of operations throughout the south relied on a maneuverist approach. We did not want to be fixed in any one location but did need to be seen by the people and provide a security bubble throughout our area of responsibility. Without enough troops to do this from static locations, we had to move around. By doing this we increased the effect that our troops on the ground could achieve. This concept of operations had been pioneered by the Australians in Vietnam where, by refusing to be fixed to bases, they could patrol large regions more effectively. We did the same. Not ideal, but that was our reality. In a sense we were spinning plates; whenever a plate started wobbling, we would get it spinning again, then move to the next wobbling plate.

We used forward operating bases as staging areas for our maneuverist approach. These FOBs allowed us to position our supplies forward, carry out maintenance and allow our troops to rest. We were frugal about how many of these bases we operated, but we did need some to cope with the enormous lines of communication we had to maintain. We had set up FOB Martello just east of Gumbad for precisely this reason. Martello helped us establish a presence in the northern part of Kandahar Province, and served as a staging site for the Dutch who deployed to Uruzgan. We had other FOBs throughout the province. One was in the south near Spin Boldak. Patrol Base Wilson in Zhari District gave us a strong presence on Highway 1. Another housed the provincial reconstruction team in Kandahar.

Whenever we assigned one of our Canadian task force companies a region to patrol, it would be staged out of one of these FOBs, but never allowed to stay in an area for long. We moved soldiers around throughout their tour so that they would stay sharp and not get too complacent in any one area. Combat operations also necessitated that we rotate troops so as to not overly tire out any one company in intense operations. This philosophy was embraced across RC South, particularly by the British in Helmand and the Dutch in Uruzgan. Other parts of the region were covered by the U.S. special forces with their own unique protocols.

But back to Mike Wright and A Company. As part of the handover from Task Force Orion to Task Force 3-06, Ian Hope had taken Omer Lavoie and Mike to the district centre in Bazar-e-Panjwayi, a major market town just north of M'sūm Ghar. There they had met the head of an Afghan special police unit by the name of Captain Massoud, one of Asadullah Khalid's boys. Captain Massoud ran a special team that reported directly to Khalid and functioned as the governor's mini-militia unit. He also worked closely and openly with the Canadians. We grew to admire him.

When Mike met Captain Massoud again on August 19, the day of the transfer of command ceremony from Ian Hope to Omer Lavoie, Mike reported that A Company had lately observed increasingly intense firefights along the high features of M'sūm Ghar from their position up at Patrol Base Wilson, five kilometres to the north. On the previous night, as journalists filed their stories from the internet tent at the patrol base, A Company had noted significant fire to the south, with tracer rounds clearly visible in the night sky. This was new. At 0200 a rocket screamed over the base, narrowly missing its intended coalition target. Clearly, the Taliban were itching for a fight.

Massoud confirmed that his officers were well aware of the activity. Taliban fighters had been exchanging fire with contingents of both the Afghan National Army and Afghan National Police and were doing so at M'sūm Ghar as they spoke. Massoud himself would be heading back there that very day. Mike was quickly deployed with A Company to M'sūm Ghar that afternoon. There he could reinforce the Afghan troops who were taking the heat on the east side of the mountain.

Bazar-e-Panjwayi is a small community just to the west of Kandahar City. Typical of an Afghan community adjacent to any city, it comprises a market and town centre and is associated with one of the hundreds of tribes in the region. Families usually live in communal home compounds. A compound will have a wall around it with several dwellings inside. The outside will be nondescript but inside the homes are adorned with colour. Children often played outside and there was a sense of normalcy that defied the dangers lurking around the corner in the form of a suicide bomber, suicide vehicle or Taliban ambush. Soldiers had to keep their wits about them, not only for the sake of their lives but also those of the innocent people in places like Bazar-e-Panjwayi.

The Afghan National Army (ANA) was the only truly national force in Afghanistan. It comprised soldiers from every region and every tribe, and they deployed all across their country. They had been fighting for years against the Taliban. While lightly equipped compared to us, they were equally equipped to the Taliban and over time became better equipped. And the Afghan people generally had a good impression of the ANA, unlike the Afghan National Police (ANP). When we arrived, however, the ANA varied hugely in capability. This was in large part due to inconsistent leadership, and this was an issue we made sure to address. We always paired up with an Afghan unit, and operated with them for the most part. We attempted to put them first. Despite this, the usefulness of the ANA during our operations was limited at best. There were exceptions of course, and the ANA matured during our tenure. I visited the region two more times after my tour, and I was very much impressed with the progress and improved capability of the ANA.

Mike remembers the event in detail:

I left a platoon to remain at Patrol Base Wilson to secure the
Zhari district centre there. I was uncertain how much space
there actually was in M'sūm Ghar, so I gave orders for 3 Platoon
to deploy with me, my artillery forward observation officer and
my LAV captain, and I put 2 Platoon on standby to come down
to Panjwayi once I assessed the situation.

As I was the only one who had previously been in the area
of Bazar-e-Panjwayi, I led the convoy of five LAVs and three jeeps
myself past the town and out to M'sūm Ghar in the late afternoon. The road leading from the district centre to the mountain
was narrow, very narrow. Halfway through, the back wheels of
my LAV slipped down into a *wadi*. Eventually all our vehicles
made it around, and I gave initial orders where to position them
before I went to meet with Captain Massoud.

Massoud was quite a character, identifiable in the field
not by an Afghan security forces uniform but rather by his
Dolce & Gabbana hat and the designer walkie-talkie he used to
communicate with his forces. When I arrived, he pointed out
the positions of his men and some observation posts on the high
ground, and we spoke about where he thought the main Taliban
thrust was coming from.

We could hear gunfire in the grape fields to the south, but
Massoud wasn't concerned. I assigned the best vantage point to
my forward observation officer, because what I was really hoping
to accomplish was for him to be able to observe what we believed
was the origin point of the mortars and rockets that had been
harassing us throughout the month, and then to neutralize them.

I placed 3 Platoon in an open area and instructed them to
link up with the Afghan police who were sprinkled around the
position. Finally, I instructed my LAV captain to go back around
the bend of M'sūm Ghar to watch our six o'clock and to secure

the route to the district centre. I then sat down on a rock to write confirmatory orders.

Five minutes later I heard a pop and looked up. A rocket-propelled grenade was heading right for me. It landed some ten feet behind my position but did not detonate. Lucky. The RPG had been fired from the high feature, which was now occupied by figures in black clothing. Machine-gun fire and RPGs continued to be directed toward us. A number of Afghan police then ran down the embankment toward 3 Platoon. To this day I credit the strong discipline of my soldiers for not firing on them by mistake. Clearly the fight was now on.

We had arrived in M'sūm Ghar just prior to a major attack by the Taliban, who were likely aiming to seize the high feature and then overtake the district centre itself. As 3 Platoon had almost no time to prepare, their soldiers took cover in the LAVs and behind whatever structures they could find. The platoon then fought the insurgents for three straight hours. The size of the force that attacked us is uncertain. The Governor of Kandahar said later it had been around 400 fighters, but Afghan math is not an exact science. The total was more likely somewhere between 100 and 150 men.

Luckily my LAV captain Mike Reekie had gone a little bit further than the 200 metres or so behind me I'd assumed he had. When he got there, he realized he couldn't see beyond the rise and advanced 200 metres more. He still couldn't see, so he moved still further, ending up on a rise close to the Taliban attack position. There he observed successive groups of eight to ten Taliban dressed in black crossing the road to scale M'sūm Ghar yet again and continue the assault in the last light of day. We engaged them.

Realizing that his viewing attachment wasn't working, Mike's driver Corporal Chad Chevrefils popped open his hatch in order to help identify targets.

What that LAV crew did that night was absolutely pivotal. Displaying superb judgment, Mike and "Chevy," as we called him—along with Mike's crew commander Sergeant Dan Holley—assessed the changing tactical situation and constantly repositioned their vehicle to maximum advantage, enabling the interception and defeat of a numerically superior enemy force during the ensuing firefight. Their outstanding initiative prevented the enemy from outflanking our position. Both later received Canada's Medal of Military Valour for their bravery, and the rest of the crew were mentioned in dispatches.

As Mike Reekie sent reports back to me about the size of the attacking force, I relayed that information to our commander back at Kandahar Airfield. Given the strength of the attack, he asked whether we needed reinforcements or even if we wanted to consider withdrawing. The answer to the first question was easy. Given the difficulty we'd had coming onto the position during the day, the limited space and the chaotic situation, I recommended against sending reinforcements. The second question was more difficult. On one hand, it was the beginning of the tour. The battlegroup was just starting operations, and we were in a pretty fierce fight against a much larger enemy than we'd expected. On the other hand, and I have to be perfectly honest here, we had a lot of regimental pride. We were a PPCLI company working with an RCR battalion. As long as I judged we could handle the fight, there would be no way we were going to pull off of that position.

After a couple of hours, we started to run low on ammunition, so I called 2 Platoon forward from Patrol Base Wilson to conduct ammunition resupply. With the fighting dying down, we then made a plan to pull off of the position and link with them in Bazar-e-Panjwayi.

Direction came to coordinate our withdrawal with the Afghan National Police. Given that I'd been in the LAV on the radio directing the fight and trying to assess the situation, I hadn't paid attention to what our Afghan allies were up to, but it turns out they'd already pulled out of the position back toward the district centre.

Finally, when it came time to withdraw to regroup and re-focus our forces, 3 Platoon's G-wagens (the short form of the German *Geländewagen*, meaning cross-country vehicle) wouldn't start. As a few remaining Taliban positions were still firing at us, the situation was tense. Yet Warrant Officer Mike Jackson and Master Corporal Paul Monroe ran the operation with cool heads, as their subsequent Medals of Military Valour attested. Fully exposed to the violence of the enemy, they got our personnel and damaged vehicles out of there. Their heroism under constant fire enabled us to regroup and continue the fight, while denying the enemy any chance of capturing and making use of our stricken equipment. We eventually withdrew from M'sūm Ghar and linked up with 2 Platoon. Thanks to a Predator strike, they had themselves narrowly missed being ambushed on their way into town. They then conducted an ambush of their own on a Taliban reinforcement party.

We were redistributing ammo when the order came to move toward contacts close to the river. I'd been down that route briefly in the daylight and was uneasy about moving along such a narrow road at night. Sure enough, as we moved in, one of the LAVs flipped onto its side. As a section dismounted from the vehicle to assess the situation, machine-gun fire sprayed down on us from a few hundred metres away. We responded, neutralizing those who were firing at us. Even as we did that, we received more reports of contacts closer to the river and began to get a picture of a very large Taliban force. As Sergeant Vince Adams was leading the operation to get the LAV back on its wheels, I assessed the situation. It was precarious, in part because of the terrain, in part because of our uncertainty about the size and the disposition of the enemy, and in part because we'd already been fighting in darkness for several hours. With Omer Lavoie's agreement, we withdrew to the outskirts of town.

As dawn was breaking, we received orders to go back to the district centre to help evacuate some Afghan police casualties. I went in with a couple of vehicles and it was eerily quiet. We saw Taliban bodies lying in the middle of the street, some with sheets over them, some uncovered. If it'd been later in the tour, I would have realized how rare it is to see a Taliban body at all; they always recover their dead quickly. We moved slowly past them, then linked up with the Afghan National Police in the district centre. They loaded their walking wounded into trucks, and we escorted them into Kandahar City.

The next day, the *Globe and Mail* reported that seventy-two Taliban had been killed.

MIKE WRIGHT

Of all the company commanders in our task force, Mike Wright was the best. Gifted with a tactical touch, he undertook his duties with a rare and powerful combination of knowledge and instinct. His leadership in Afghanistan set the standard to which all other officers aspired. Great credit too goes to the men and women of the Royal Canadian Regiment, who welcomed Mike and his team so openly. Without doubt, our battlegroup commander Omer Lavoie and his regimental sergeant major, Chief Warrant Officer Bobby Girouard, deserve credit for ensuring that regimental differences would play no role in the battalion and in the operation. Together they set a tone of open collaboration that created one team and one team only. We all play for Canada.

With the full support of the larger battlegroup, A Company was able to conduct extremely successful high-intensity combat operations over the first three months of the tour, and also to ratchet down to focus on the critical activities of capacity-building and reconstruction. On August 19 and 20, the 126 soldiers of A Company had represented their battalion and their regiment well. Within two weeks, they would be called upon to do so again under even greater pressure.

Mike Wright (top centre, holding the A Company pennant) joined the 2nd Battalion as a lieutenant and was immediately spotted as an officer with potential. He was commanding A Company with 2 PPCLI when he was attached to 1 RCR for Afghanistan. I credit Omer Lavoie and his command team for making the integration into 1 RCR as easy as possible for Mike and his company. Mike's own personality made this possible too. Mike is a quiet and highly proficient officer with a wicked sense of humour. He can be tough and funny when the situation requires. It was a pleasure to see Mike again and watch his stellar performance in Afghanistan. Mike's first engagement, days after arriving, occurred south of M'sūm Ghar where he bumped into a sizeable Taliban attacking force. The gun battle that ensued lasted hours until Mike was able to defeat them. Mike received the Medal of Bravery for his actions during this opening battle, which was a fitting testament to his amazing leadership skills.

CHAPTER 11

PLAN

All the men in the Posse are true warriors, men I consider to
be brothers. I love them all dearly.

MOTHER

O nce the idea was clear in my mind, I called the commander of ISAF, David Richards. "Here's the situation," I
said. "I have to be unconventional about this, so it's going
to be a long, drawn-out process. We've created a four-phase plan
that has some dates on it, but those timings are loose. The decisions
to move from one phase to another will be based on conditions, not
calendars."

We couldn't anticipate how the Taliban would react to our plans.
We had a notion of what we could do to them with each action, but
the proof would come only as events unfolded. Medusa was to be an
effects-based operation. I wanted my team to be agile enough to take
advantage of the situation on the ground. I would not limit us to fixed
timelines, and instead would work with my planners to set down a
number of conditions—which, if and when realized, would trigger
other actions. This approach would give us the flexibility to gain and
maintain the initiative as things changed.

We foresaw four distinct phases of activity:

1. Shape
2. Strike

3. Exploit

4. Stabilize.

Originally, we had expected Phase 1 to run until mid to late September, by which time Ben Freakley and his RC East brigade commander John Nicholson would be done with the air assets and other enablers we needed. That would all change on August 19, when a pivotal meeting with Governor Khalid would change our entire understanding of the situation in Panjwayi. More on that later. For now, I'll just say that until that moment, we thought we had weeks before launching our strike phase. Now we had days. On August 22 during Phase 1 — Shape — ISAF's priorities changed. David Richards quickly agreed to make Operation Medusa NATO's main effort in Afghanistan. Ben Freakley immediately reassigned all his assets to RC South. We would have his aircraft, weapons and additional troops to guarantee the force ratios necessary for our single battalion to go up against the largest Taliban force ever assembled. But we would have those only for the first two or three weeks of September, after which the balance of power in RC East might swing to the Taliban factions there.

While Medusa would be the main effort for RC South from late August into September, the operation would represent a mere third of our activity. We had an undeniable duty to keep concurrent pressure on the Taliban throughout the rest of the region. As we would soon learn, as we fought Operation Medusa we would also deal with no fewer than sixty other TICs and be forced to maintain an operational tempo accelerated daily by a steady stream of competing requirements. While managing the replacement of 3 PARA by the Royal Marines, our British task force in Helmand would keep fighting in Sangin, Kajaki and Musa Qala. The Romanians would take over from the Americans over in Zabul. Special Forces would execute operations every day in every province. We would actively support local communities in Afghan development zones across Zabul and Helmand provinces. ISAF headquarters would continually ask for data on police patrols completed, hospitals supported, key leaders engaged, roofs repaired, markets opened, and on and on. As such, our story was to be one not just of courage under pressure but also, and perhaps as heroic, one of managing the complexity, contradiction, confusion and chaos thrown at us from every direction. Every organization involved had its own unique and often conflicting perspectives, needs and priorities. Paradoxically, of everything we had to deal with, the Taliban would be the only straightforward factor.

The intent of Operation Medusa was to defeat the Taliban in the vicinity of Zhari and Panjwayi in order to maintain freedom of movement along Highway 1 and uphold the security of Kandahar City. If we managed that, we could set the necessary precondition for the establishment of the Kandahar Afghan Development Zone (ADZ), which would soon bolster the local economy, return these districts to some normalcy and prove to the locals that, supported by the NATO coalition, their elected authorities in the government of Afghanistan could offer a better long-term solution to their troubles than siding with the insurgents. But if we dragged our feet and if villagers in these districts sided with the Taliban, Kandahar would surely fall.

It was as though we had been planning an operation in some backwater Ontario town and had just learned we were about to lose Toronto to the enemy.

Our priorities were threefold. First, we wanted to demonstrate to locals that NATO's commitment to the area was real, and that its capability to make a difference was high. Second, we would try to get local leaders to assist us and the Afghan National Army with our actions in Pashmul. We learned this aim was at immediate risk if we didn't progress quickly to Phase 2 — Strike. Third, we wanted to get the message across to less committed Taliban fighters that it was time to surrender or die.

In our plan, we all had specific conditions to watch for. For example, once H-Hour, our start time, was declared and the operation was underway, and if Charles Company detected no fire south of the Arghandab riverbank, they would immediately move to establish a bridgehead in the vicinity of the white schoolhouse, oriented north. If and when our own troops on the southern flank were threatened and resourceless, I would deploy our first-echelon reserve to assist. If certain defined objectives were successfully secured, A Company would clear the route to the next ones. If and when we assessed that enemy strength had been reduced by 75 per cent, our battlegroup would send in companies from opposite sides to squeeze the remaining Taliban and link up.

Each unit knew what to do, and had a specific role to play and a long set of actions to carry out on particular objectives at anticipated moments. These were detailed in a brilliantly concise synchronization matrix, a two-page document that presented Operation Medusa at a glance.

A critical element of our Phase 1 activity was coordinating all our intelligence, surveillance and reconnaissance (ISR) assets to prepare for the battle. Their job was target development. This meant the tracking of high-value and medium-value targets within the areas we had designated as objectives. And there were many. In Pashmul alone, we identified eighteen locations that required constant monitoring, including leadership and communication posts, IED factories, mortar installations, medical stations, supply caches, supply routes, ambush sites, and even likely nearby spots from which Taliban scouts could give early warning of our arrival. We would use a protocol called F2T2EA, a beefy acronym for the six discrete steps we take to find, fix, track, target and engage the enemy and assess the effect created. As we did that, our ISR assets would be feeding NATO troops on the ground the increased situational awareness they needed to move deliberately and effectively onto each objective.

Based upon an assessment of all that intelligence, we developed a template. Then we kept evolving it based upon the situation on the ground and further intelligence reports. From this we assigned the various objectives, which for this operation took the names of sports:

Rugby, Tennis, Lacrosse, Cricket, Baseball and so on. We then assigned named areas of interest (NAI), on top of which we put air assets to develop, i.e. to confirm or revise what we thought was there.

The shaping portion of the battle was in part to validate the template before we attacked. In that first phase, we would also make sure everything was working and coordinated properly, and we would move into the rhythm of building and sharing daily reports of enemy placements, movements and capability.

Using our full combination of intelligence assets, including our network of friendly local nationals, we could track exactly where and when Taliban commanders were setting up their headquarters. We watched and listened. We learned that Mullah Abdul Hanan had taken a position far south of the Arghandab River—in Talukan, just above the Red Desert. As the Taliban's senior commander for central Kandahar, Hanan was brought in as a kind of brigade commander to run the whole defensive operation. From his command post in Talukan he would dispatch thirty-man fighting cells into Pashmul and rotate them out to Servan and Zangabad as needed for rest and refit. Listening in on Hanan's communications, we learned that he intended to fight us with a combination of IEDs, mortars and ambushes, and eventually full-on assaults.

Hanan controlled his next-in-command Haji Lala, who was installed across the Arghandab from his boss not far from Siah Choy. (Lala had been one of the tribal leaders at that pivotal meeting at Khalid's house.) In charge of tactics, Lala was the Taliban equivalent of a battalion commander, controlling as many as five sub-commanders, who each gave orders to three twenty- or thirty-man cells. Those guys— including Kaka Abdul Khaliq, Mullah Gul Agha and Amir Sabar Mohammand—were effectively the Taliban's company commanders. I mention their names only to show that our intel was detailed. We already knew, for instance, that Amir Sabar Mohammand was in place just under Sperwan Ghar on the south of the river, and that, while ready to reinforce Pashmul with fresh fighters as needed, he in no way welcomed the prospect of fighting on his side of the river as he didn't have enough troops there. We tucked that fact away for later.

What was important for us was our growing understanding that the Taliban were abandoning their typically lean chain of command. With their brigade commander, battalion commander and company commanders, their span-of-control model was beginning to look a lot like ours. Here again, they were swinging from insurgent to conventional warfare.

We could watch and listen to them with our sophisticated array of intelligence and surveillance systems. In the air we had Predators, long-endurance drones that fed line-of-sight video to us in real time. We had Sperwar, French-built unmanned aerial vehicles that could send target images back from as far as 150 kilometres away. Other platforms collected data from ultra-high altitudes, while British Nimrod aircraft conducted aerial surveillance. On the ground, other assets gathered intelligence on the Taliban as well. From that intelligence we drew assumptions, and with our assumptions we made plans.

But planning is more art than science.

We often made assumptions that were wrong. We hadn't yet realized that M'sūm Ghar itself would be overrun with Taliban. So close to Kandahar, it was like finding a wasp's nest on our porch. We would deal with that surprise later, but I mention it now because it made us aware that intel is always possibly wrong, possibly incomplete. You can base a plan in part on intel, but you'd better be ready to change it twenty seconds after you put that plan it into action.

For one thing, every student of military history knows to expect trickery. The smartest tactic each side can use is to fill the enemy's intelligence network with false information. Every day I reminded my officers that we now had "a clear picture of the enemy situation with a plus or minus 100 per cent chance of error." Phase 1 — Shape — would be like the opening moves of a chess game, where expert players shift pieces ambiguously to confuse the opposition about their intent. As they feint, they look to see how the other side reacts and, more to the point, what the other side is failing to consider. They tease the enemy to reveal itself. They look for weaknesses. And that was exactly what I intended to do.

The Taliban were hard to find but easy to kill. As we pounded the enemy in Phase 1, we would watch until we saw them and detected a so-called pattern of life. Every time they poked their heads up, we'd chop those heads off and watch what happened. We'd do it over and over and over until they started making stupid mistakes. That's how we

The key to operations is intelligence, surveillance and reconnaissance. Without knowing what is out there, you will never have good situational awareness. Canada bought the Sperwar, an unmanned aerial vehicle manufactured by SAGEM in France. Sperwar relayed images of possible targets to us back on the ground. The mere sound of the Sperwer flying overhead made many Canadian soldiers comfortable that they had eyes on target. This was a critical enabler that we used extensively in addition to its bigger cousin, the Predator. Why the Canadian air force did not invest in this capability sooner defies logic. Nowhere today will any commander send out troops without access to a UAV. This little bird was certainly loved by every soldier on the ground, who could see what was around them. The surveillance pod on this aircraft was one of the best we could obtain.

would shape the battlespace. Once their command and control was fully lit up, once they were confused, fatigued and as close as I thought they would get to combat ineffectiveness, I would start Phase 2 — Strike — and we'd go in and kill as many of them as we could.

At that point and only at that point, we would revert to conventional protocols. We would advance objective-by-objective, deploying our troops just as we had in the Second World War and in the Korean War, but this time with much better surveillance and air power. The condition I would be waiting to confirm was not complicated: I simply wanted to be sure they were tired. After that, we'd finish them off.

That would be Phase 3, when we exploited our advantage. We'd be mopping them up, clearing the area of every last fighter. When that was done, and only when that was done, we could get to Phase 4 and begin stabilizing the region. We'd encourage displaced residents to come back to their homes, launch an ambitious program of projects with our partners in order to rebuild anything that had been destroyed or damaged, put our provincial reconstruction teams back to work building new infrastructure, and allow the Afghan army and the police to take a more dominant role in security. With the Taliban gone, we would finally be able to get on with our actual mission.

That was the plan I sent early in the second week of August to David Richards and Ben Freakley in Kabul, and to Mike Gauthier and Rick Hillier in Ottawa. I told them frankly that when we launched, the operation would probably look good for the first couple of days, even the first week, but after that it would seem dragged out. They would start being put under incredible political pressure to get the thing over and done with, but there was no way I could put a reliable timeline on our execution of this campaign. We may make the plan, but the enemy gets a vote.

CHAPTER 12

ACCELERATE

After we got hit, the Boss saw me and said, "We gotta talk." He
got in the turret, put his hand on his face and just looked at me
for a long time. No words. I broke down, bawling. I wanted to go
home. He said, "I'll send you home, but we've got guys here who
need you. This is your decision point." I stayed.

MOTHER

Until writing this book, I had not fully grasped that the need to
change the timing, tempo and tenor of Operation Medusa had
arisen at one bizarre meeting at the residence of the Governor
of Kandahar. A meeting I wasn't even there for.

Here's the background. Operation Enduring Freedom began
as an American operation but from the outset was structured to
make way for an International Security Assistance Force (ISAF)
to start taking over operations as early as 2002. The process was
designed in slow, measured stages, with the turnover of Regional
Command South scheduled for July 31, 2006. During the first half
of that year, everyone in Afghanistan knew that command of international forces would shift from the Americans to ISAF. They also
knew the Taliban were gearing up to try their luck against the NATO
rookies.

In the meantime, Ben Freakley and his brigade commander John
Nicholson were going head-to-head with Taliban in Regional
Command East, an area slightly smaller than Nova Scotia, and one

that U.S. senator Joe Biden had famously dubbed the most dangerous place on earth. Obviously he had never visited RC South.

As the July 31 turnover in RC South approached, Freakley knew he had limited time to use the considerable air and ground assets at his disposal to settle matters in RC East before the Taliban turned their attention to Kandahar.

> After that, RC South could have access to all those critical enablers, all those force multipliers, probably somewhere around the end of September or early October. That was the assumption we worked under. It's why we planned Medusa as more of a staged event, with the kinetic Phase 2 (Strike) not starting until we had all those enablers at our disposal.
>
> SHANE SCHREIBER

By mid-August, Omer Lavoie's 1st Battalion, The Royal Canadian Regiment had arrived in Kandahar, and the transfer of command on Saturday, August 19 had Omer take over the Task Force 3-06 battle-group. Till then that group had been known as Task Force Orion, commanded by Ian Hope and centred around his own 1st Battalion, Princess Patricia's Canadian Light Infantry. Everything was ticking along as planned. Then Governor Asadullah Khalid called a meeting.

Governor Khalid was a rebel and difficult to work with. Early in 2006, we had rated him as effective, but that assessment would change. He always played for his own gain. To shore up his power base, he kept two advisors inside his tent. The first was Mullah Naqib, the tribal elder for Arghandab District who was incredibly influential, having come into notoriety for pushing the Soviets out of his area. In particular he was known for taking out three Russian tanks with his own RPG and then personally executing thirty Russian soldiers, apparently with some relish. His district never had problems with the Taliban, because Mullah Naqib gave them full, free and unquestioned transit through his territory to places like Panjwayi. They could bring all the troops, weapons and munitions they wanted across his turf, and no doubt be well fed and quartered as they did. Governor Khalid relied on Mullah Naqib for many reasons: he had constant access to the Taliban leadership, he was already bent and therefore manipulable, and he would happily lie to anyone.

Ahmed Wali Karzai was his other close confederate. Wali was one of President Hamid Karzai's three brothers and had served as a key ally to the U.S. military in the south of Afghanistan from the moment they arrived. He too was corrupt and under the active surveillance of other organizations—who, rumour had it, were paying him to get things done when it suited them. An entrepreneur—as much as anyone on the take who double-deals and uses public money to pay off his friends could be dubbed entrepreneurial—Wali Karzai also strong-armed his way into the position of chairman of the Kandahar Provincial Council. He used that position to his advantage from 2005 until his own head of security assassinated him with one pistol shot to the head and one to the chest in July 2011. No one was surprised; it was the ninth assassination attempt against Wali in as many years.

So with Mullah Naqib and Wali Karzai as close advisors and co-conspirators, Governor Asadullah Khalid felt untouchable. But he, like so many, had a weak spot—unquenchable ambition. He wanted as much power as Wali's now-famous brother Hamid, and to get it he knew he would have to land a plum job in Kabul one day. I knew that about him. Once, when we were at a meeting with Khalid and his retinue listening to a load of political doublespeak that screamed *do it our way or else*, I'd had enough. Khalid was trying to get us to hire his own police for our security, thereby putting his henchmen where they could watch us and report. He could then pass on our plans to the Taliban. It was a clumsy attempt at infiltration and, as soon as he made the suggestion, I drew him aside for a private word. I don't recall if I asked everyone to leave the room or just led him down the hall to his own office, but no guards, no police and no interpreters were present. I told him, "Enough of this bullshit, Khalid. You think you're tough,

Governor Asadullah Khalid was a young, ambitious and well-connected politician. He was close to the Karzai family (Hamid Karzai was president of the country at the time) and ran the province out of his pockets. He had numerous cell phones that he would answer any time they rang (even in meetings), and he would often run off because of what he'd been told in the call. When I first met him, it was not uncommon for him to charge out of the office, jump into his suv and head straight into some firefight with his AK-47. That was simply how he did business. He could speak very good English and had business dealings in the U.S. Khalid was probably a businessman more than he was a politician. He was always working on the margins, which made things more difficult than they should have been; however, he had energy and wanted to get things done. That was important, and we did get a lot done. Khalid was inexperienced, but he was smart enough to learn from the advice he was given by the small circle of tribal advisors he had around him. Only once did I have to inter- vene and explain to him the way things were going to be. We did this with just him and me, ensuring he never lost face with the team, and after that meeting we worked well together. He was one of those individuals you liked, though you knew that he was somewhat grey and you needed to keep a finger on him. He was the future of the country and he needed to be allowed the time to grow, which he did. But you could never take your eye off him.

but I'm Dave Fraser and I'm the biggest, meanest warlord in this part of the country. I've got more men, more weapons and more ammunition than you'll see in your whole miserable life. I know you're corrupt. But I have friends everywhere. I can stop you from getting any position in Kabul you could ever dream of having. So no more busting NATO's balls down here. Agreed?"

And he agreed. After that, while we never trusted him, he never gave us any more trouble. In return, we never let him lose face in public. Tit for tat.

On August 17 and 18 I had hunkered down with my assistant chief of operations Shane Schreiber and our planning team to go over our plan for Operation Medusa in detail. We were already in the middle of Phase 1, shaping the battle by playing whack-a-mole. The Taliban were the moles, and our artillery was the mallet. We were still tracking a likely start date for decisive ops some time in mid to late September. While we had been given priority of resources (read air cover) through August (mostly because of the countrywide change from Operation Enduring Freedom to NATO, and local turnovers including the Canadian task force in Kandahar, the British task force in Helmand and the Romanian task force in Zabul)—that was for that month only. Remember, back then we were still thinking that in September, those resources would be swung back to RC East for their own offensive operation against the Taliban. But we knew we had three or four more weeks in the first phase of Medusa to play whack-a-mole with the enemy, collect intelligence, get Omer's troops in shape, rally the political and tribal leaders, prepare the population and continue detailed planning for the upcoming combat phase.

My plan was to attend the transfer of command authority (TOCA) ceremony on August 19, in which Omer Lavoie and the RCR would relieve Ian Hope and his PPCLI, then shoot up to Kabul to brief Generals Richards and Freakley, the ISAF Regional Assessment Board and the Canadian Advisory Team. That done, I'd head to Ottawa to brief the Minister of National Defence on what we were up to. I'd also have time to brief General Mike Gauthier, Rick Hillier and Prime Minister Harper on the upcoming operation, and then attend two change-of-command ceremonies in Edmonton two days later.

After the TOCA, I jumped on a plane to Bagram and was gone. That afternoon, Ian and Omer came over to the RC South headquarters and met our deputy commander Steve Williams, chief of staff Chris Vernon and Shane Schreiber. At around 1400 hours they received an urgent invitation from Governor Khalid to be in his compound by 1700, so they fired up Ian and Omer's TAC and convoyed into Kandahar. I'll let Shane tell the story.

> We got there on time. There with the governor was Haji Lala, the chief of one of the local Panjwayi tribes who, our intelligence had confirmed, was a senior Taliban commander. Beside him were other tribal elders including Haji Amitullah, a man we strongly suspected to have Taliban affiliations of his own. Wali Karzai showed up later. It was a weird vibe. People we knew to be traitors were sitting right there smiling at us.
>
> The governor got to the point. He opened by saying, "I understand that you have heard that my friend Haji Amitullah is making a deal with the Taliban." All of us on the RC South staff expected the governor to now deny that allegation and vouch for his friend. Instead he said, "Friends, I am here to tell you what you have heard is absolutely true."
>
> Boom.
>
> There was a moment of stunned silence and disbelief. The Governor of Kandahar had just outed Amitullah in our presence, essentially signing this guy's death warrant. It was a bit of a brain-grenade. He went on: "Some of these other leaders are also speaking to the Taliban."
>
> Double boom.
>
> "They are talking to the Taliban because the Americans are leaving, and ISAF says it won't fight because ISAF is here just for

Omer Lavoie and I had never met before the Afghanistan mission. He joined my brigade during our operational evaluation and shadowed 1 PPCLI. Following that, he was fed our reports from theatre as he prepared his unit to take over from Ian Hope's task force. When I met Omer again, it was during the handover in theatre and it was one of the busiest transitions we had during our tour. Omer was operationally experienced and passionate about his unit. He had done much to get ready for the mission, but nothing could have prepared him for the tempo that he faced when he arrived. His 1 RCR did not have the opportunity for acclimatizing in theatre like other units. They were put to the test immediately. Omer was ably assisted by one of the best regimental sergeant majors I have seen, Bobby Girouard, as well as his deputy Marty Lipcsey and some good company commanders. 1 RCR, up until then a battle-untested formation, had to learn on the job, so to speak. It took its toll on Omer, who felt the weight of command because of his love for his soldiers. Nevertheless, he did it and the unit was successful—albeit at a terrible cost. Command is a lonely position, and for Omer it was more lonely given that he arrived at the height of the biggest battle we would fight during our tour.

Shane Schreiber was my brigade chief of staff when I took over 1 CMBG. He essentially ran the staff and ensured everything was coordinated. Never have I met someone as smart or brilliant as Shane. He was well read, could write like no one else and had a work ethic that was commendable. I was thrilled to have him as my COS. He was well liked by all and was a focal point in the HQ. Shane never showed he was feeling the pressures of the job and was always good working with people, even when they needed a kick. He had a way of getting the most out of everyone. He was my go-to guy. I think if we had not had Shane, our operations would not have been as effective. The operational tempo we had trained for paled in comparison to the real thing, and Shane managed all of this with apparent ease. It was his intellect coupled with his work ethic that made the impossible possible. He did make me laugh many times. During our operational training mission in Wainwright, we had planned a complex brigade operation—"a symphony in five acts." During the night, someone higher up changed something, trying to make it easier for us, but the reality was that it undid all of our preparations for the next day. At about 0200, Shane told the staff to wake me up because this was going to take my intervention and approval. He sent Darcy Hedon, one of our great officers, to do the honours, reasoning that I wouldn't growl at being awakened by Darcy, whereas I might if it were Shane. Smart move.

rebuilding. So the Taliban are telling the people that they alone have been left to look after security in Kandahar. If that is true, what choice do my friends have but to make deals with the Taliban?"

Triple boom.

Chris Vernon asked calmly, "What makes you think ISAF won't fight?"

The governor then alluded to an ISAF information campaign surrounding the recent launch of the Afghan Development Zone concept promoted by General David Richards. He shot back, "That's precisely what you, ISAF, are telling us. You are here for development and not for fighting. Here . . . read what you said."

Quadruple boom.

A vigorous conversation ensued in which both the will and the capability of ISAF to take on the Taliban were more than questioned, they were openly denied. To demonstrate RC South's commitment, Chris Vernon explained the concept of operations for Medusa, which had already received endorsement from the Afghan government in Kabul and this very governor in Kandahar. ISAF was about to demonstrate its will and capability to defeat the Taliban on the doorstep of his city. We would produce a demonstration of firepower that the people of Kandahar could not help but see. It would be a highly public destruction of the Taliban, just like a showdown at high noon in a Western movie.

That raised an eyebrow or two.

"One concern from ISAF's perspective," I pointed out, "is the strong likelihood of collateral damage. RC South and coalition forces have been roundly condemned for the level of such damage inflicted on locals. We've been criticized by President Karzai, by you, Governor, and by other officials." They didn't know as we did that the damage in question had been inflicted largely by special operations forces and not our brigade. But we knew that taking on the Taliban in a conventional fight would risk significant collateral damage. "I guarantee you," I said, "that we are going to break your compounds and smash a lot of stuff trying to get at the Taliban, so you'll have to find a way to not criticize us for taking the measures you're asking for."

The governor and many of the other tribal elders in the room nodded their heads. One who had not yet spoken said, "Go ahead and break what you must. We cannot live in our homes. We cannot use our compounds with the Taliban there. It is all useless to us. If you must destroy it to drive out the Taliban, so be it."

Chris Vernon added, "You must move your people out of harm's way. No one will be safe from the firepower we're going to throw at this." The Afghans looked at each other and came to a quick agreement. "We will get them out of the way. We will bring them to the city or elsewhere to make sure that they are safe."

To the conventional military mind, warning the public (and therefore the enemy) of an impending attack is an egregious violation of operational security, but we had to do it. We agreed to publicly inform both locals and Taliban that they had two weeks to leave the area. Anyone left in Pashmul or Zhari would thereafter be considered an enemy and be destroyed. To maintain operational security and keep the Taliban guessing, we wouldn't say exactly when or from which direction we were coming, but by God we were coming.

The meeting went on with some great lines being spoken. Steve Williams, our American deputy commander, gleefully promised Haji Lala that he would walk hand-in-hand with him over "the smashed rubble of Pashmul" as Christina Green, our Canadian CIDA rep at the far end of the room, quietly went pale. Haji turned to me and in a breathless whisper asked, "Did the American just promise to destroy the village to save it?" "Not quite," I answered. "I think he meant to say that by the time we are done, Pashmul will be safe enough to walk around without any fear of the Taliban. But yes, also a bit damaged."

We got back to RC South headquarters around 2100. I quickly wrote up a meeting report explaining to ISAF headquarters that this was "ISAF's last, best chance to demonstrate not just ISAF's capability, but more importantly its will to defeat the Taliban in the vital province of Kandahar." I had Chris Vernon review it and then sent it to ISAF HQ around 2300 that night. Through the evening, Chris Vernon and I had also been on the phone to the ISAF chief of staff explaining the extraordinary meeting we'd just come from and impressing on them how Medusa was now more important than ever, not just to Kandahar and RC South, but to NATO as a whole.

SHANE SCHREIBER

I never saw Shane's report. Our email system was encrypted and secure, so after leaving headquarters at Kandahar Airfield I no longer had access. As a result of that meeting and the subsequent change in ISAF priorities, Operation Medusa's strike phase would now begin much earlier than originally scheduled—but I didn't know that until the day Rick Hillier and I were together attending the change-of-command ceremonies in Edmonton. His cell phone rang. He answered, listened quietly, then looked up and passed me the phone.

Twenty seconds later I knew I had to go back.

A key consideration as I returned was whether I would call back the members of the Posse from their leave. They had departed only a few days before, and they all deserved and needed a rest. Their families needed them too. I understood that they would be supremely annoyed with me, but their displeasure would be bearable given what they had already been through. I decided not to interrupt their break.

I was sitting at the kitchen table when my wife, Shelley, said, "Hey, Dave Fraser is on TV!" And there he was, talking about Operation Medusa. I just thought, "That sure as hell better be file footage." But a banner on the screen read LIVE FROM KANDAHAR. I blew a gasket. I stormed out to the garage, threw a

Commanders are busy people, and without a good staff around them they will simply not be able to handle the volume of work that they have to. Working as the executive assistant (EA) to a French general in Sarajevo, I learned that staff are critical in allowing generals to think, lead and provide guidance. If the general is doing more than that, the staff are not doing their jobs. When I arrived in Edmonton to take over the brigade, I had a personal assistant but no EA, which was going to be critical in theatre. I met David Buchanan during our operational evaluation exercise. He ran our ISTAR capabilities and was an artillery officer. I was so impressed with his talents, I made him my EA and said he could do any other tasks as required. It was one of my best decisions. "Buck" was my gatekeeper and managed everything that went in or out of the office. He was the source for anyone who wanted to know what I thought. Buck was a no-nonsense gunner who could manage volumes of detail with ease. He took care of everything, allowing me to think, lead and provide guidance. When Buck spoke, we all listened. He was also diplomatic in working behind the scenes to ensure that I was focused. Buck might not have been the most sociable person to others, but then again, others did not fully appreciate the burden or volume of what went on inside my office. Buck was one of the unsung heroes of this mission.

bunch of things around, then after a long time came back in the house very quiet. The Boss was deliberately keeping us out of theatre, and we couldn't do our job, which was to support and protect him. We were letting him down.

DAVID "BUCK" BUCHANAN

I was in the Maldives with my wife when I turned on BBC and saw the Boss telling the media that Operation Medusa had started. I flipped. I totally flipped. I said, "I need to be there. I'm leaving. I'm getting off this fucking island." Trina said, "What are you gonna do, swim back?"

BILL "MOTHER" IRVING

In theatre I still had some members of the Posse who had taken their leave earlier. I also had our newest close protection team member Adam Seegmiller and my personal assistant Greg Chan with me. I determined that we could use the team on hand. We would just have to scrounge transportation until the rest of the Posse came back from leave as scheduled. To this day, I am still in the doghouse for not having called everyone back.

Greg Chan was my personal assistant. A Patricia officer, he joined the Posse just before we launched Operation Medusa after five months in theatre. He proved to be one of the best officers I have ever had the pleasure to work with. He immediately fit into our team, which was a blessing as we were entering the most difficult stage of the mission. When he arrived, much of the Posse were going on a well-deserved period of leave, but then the start date for Medusa was advanced for vital strategic reasons. So at the height of the fighting, it was just Greg who had to manage the office along with everything else that was going on. He understood me completely without my having to say much. He had a great personality, anticipated our needs, coordinated effectively and did an outstanding job. We all benefited from Greg's sense of humour, which during those days was much needed and appreciated. By the end of Medusa, he was justifiably tired.

CHAPTER 13

AMASS

The career is tough on marriages. I'm on my third. At least I've
got another kick at it.

MOTHER

O n September 1, 2006 we took another urgent call from
Governor Khalid. The Afghan National Directorate of
Security, the nation's secret service, had just confirmed
multiple reports that the Taliban in Panjwayi were admitting fatigue.
We were as ready to launch Phase 2 of the operation as we'd ever be.

Our front-line force was Omer Lavoie's Task Force 3-06, comprising two companies from the first battalion of the Royal Canadian
Regiment—with Majors Matthew Sprague and Geoff Abthorpe
commanding Charles Company and Bravo Company respectively.
Omer also had Mike Wright with A Company of Princess Patricia's
Canadian Light Infantry, fresh from their August 19 all-night firefight with the Taliban on M'sūm Ghar. The battalion's regimental
sergeant major was Chief Warrant Officer Bobby Girouard, a New
Brunswick native with twenty-nine years' active military service in
Germany, Kosovo and Bosnia, and a long list of previous NATO
postings. Sniper teams had joined each of Omer's three companies
to provide precision fires as they approached each strong point.
And our in-theatre Canadian special forces were now operating in
our combined joint special operations task force under Colonel
Dave Barr.

Artillery would be the responsibility of Major Greg Ivey's E Battery of the 2nd Regiment Royal Canadian Horse Artillery. Their firepower came from four M777 howitzers, each of which packed enough punch to put a hole in a grape-drying hut—and we'd need to do a lot of that. In addition, the Dutch had loaned us two Panzerhaubitze 2000s. These German-built, 155mm self-propelled howitzers had incredibly high rates of fire; in burst mode each one could easily spit out one round every three seconds. We brigaded these north of Highway 1 in direct support of Omer's task force, giving Greg as many as six howitzers to use to torment enemy positions and support our forward operating bases.

Mark Gasparotto's 2 Combat Engineer Regiment, specifically 23 Field Squadron, would clear the countless IEDs put in the way of our advance. Each road into any of our chosen objectives would be a minefield of its own. Mark had scrounged a couple of armoured bull-dozers from contractors at Kandahar Airfield (I'm not sure how enthu-siastic they were about that), and with them he would create whole new roads as needed through un-mined areas. His teams, which included navy divers from the Fleet Diving Unit (Atlantic) in Halifax, would also remove or detonate everything in our way on existing routes. To do this they used route-clearance packages—units of three or four ingeniously designed vehicles. The first vehicle in these units was a weird-looking thing with a blast-proof, road-width bar stuffed with electronics that could detect IEDs. When that happened, it stopped, put down a little flag and backed off. A second vehicle then moved in with an elongated arm to excavate around the device. The third and sometimes fourth vehicle carried the engineering team itself, and in each case they decided how to dispose of the mine or IED.

We had two route-clearance packages in RC South. They were what we refer to as low-density assets, army jargon for things we don't have many of and that everybody wants. I had seen them first in RC East when visiting the highly sophisticated and very large counter-IED task force run by the Americans. I was immediately impressed with their combination of counter-IED exploitation and counter-IED analytics, and I knew we had to create the same capability in theatre. The Canadian army has some of the best sappers in the world, but the gear they had then was so limited in comparison it was as though we'd been asking them to clear each road by putting their fingers in their ears and stamping their feet in the dirt. I sent two people from RC South to the U.S. task force and said, "You learn everything about how they do this,

The M777 howitzer was the integral indirect gun we used to support our ground operations. This 155mm howitzer was state of the art. When we conducted our recce in August of 2005, we determined that indirect fire was essential to support ground troops. No soldier was to go outside the wire without support from an unseen artillery piece. During the recce, we determined that the 105mm howitzers Canada had planned on using would have been limited in range and ground effects. My dear friend General Andrew Leslie told me that we could acquire the U.S.-built M777 howitzer. This was a new gun and the best available. Its range and portability made it the only real option. My brigade sergeant major, Chief Warrant Officer Mike MacDonald, a master gunner, validated all our requirements, and his support of this gun further reinforced our desire to get it. The M777 ended up being extensively used and appreciated by the troops on the ground. The gunners loved it, and we moved our howitzers throughout the battlefield on the ground and by air. These guns were one of the most important combat enablers we had. No one moved without an M777 supporting them.

and while you're learning, I'll get the gear." We then wrote to Ottawa saying: *This is what we're going to do and this is what we're going to need. Send it.* Then, with Mark Gasparotto's team at the helm, we pioneered, tested and refined a whole new Canadian system of route clearance. That's the system still used throughout the Canadian army today.

General Bismillah Khan Mohammadi, the defence minister, had made sure we had all the national soldiers he could give us on behalf of the citizens of Afghanistan. After all, this was their country and their fight; we were only here to support them. We already had the 205th Corps of the Afghan National Army (ANA) fighting with us. Formed in 2004 and stationed in Kandahar, the 205th had been right beside us in all our operations across the south. They were organized as a *kandak*, the typical battalion of the ANA made up of some 600 troops. The 205th were independent from us, reporting up the Afghan chain of command, but they paired their troops with ours and followed our tempo. I acted as a mentor to their commander, Major General Rahmatullah Raufi, a solid soldier always ready to plan collaboratively. For Medusa, the 205th would be augmented by Afghan soldiers from other parts of the country who were serving with the 201st, 203rd and 209th Corps of the ANA. This highly visible commitment had a deep psychological impact on the population of the country, who could see that the Afghan army was now in the fight. It also gave a big morale boost to the Afghan army itself, which as of September had 26,900 soldiers, up 25 per cent from the year before.

In the south, Major Andrew Lussier would lead his recce squadron of a hundred soldiers, conducting intelligence, surveillance, target acquisition and reconnaissance (ISTAR). Most of his troops were Royal Canadian Dragoons, a senior cavalry regiment originally formed in 1883 to defend Canada against Fenian raiders from the United States. ISTAR teams drove around in LAV-25 vehicles fitted out with 7-metre masts housing radar and cameras. From south of the river, they could look right into Panjwayi and give us early warning of developments. They would be Omer's eyes and ears.

We had other nations involved too, although national caveats required that their involvement be severely limited. About fifty soldiers of the Netherlands' Mechanized Infantry Brigade came down from Uruzgan Province. They would conduct route protection along Highway 1, which was essential. As they drove up and down that main road, they would scare off the Taliban, thereby proving to local nationals that the insurgents had been exaggerating their power, and reassuring them that we were in charge. While the Dutch couldn't engage the enemy, their lesser role was critical to our campaign.

A reconnaissance squadron of Danes in armoured vehicles came in from the UK task force in Helmand. Their rule of engagement was simple: don't. That was disappointing. All they could do was position themselves as observers on the western flank and feed us any intel they bumped into. But Brigadier Ed Butler, commander of the UK contingent who had sent them, dug deep for us on another front. Ed and I hadn't seen eye to eye for a while, especially given the events surrounding the attack on Sangin in mid-July. But there is a code: when another soldier is down, you do not question, but rather move in to support. The UK director of special forces provided us with additional UK operators to head south and block Taliban ingress through Spin Boldak and the Red Desert. This was a huge advantage to us. As long as the Taliban couldn't get fresh troops or more ammunition, their staying power would be finite. Ed also freed up a number of Brits who could replace our own in security roles at Kandahar Airfield and FOB Martello. We also had Macedonian extras who could man the gates and get more Canadians to the front. All those fighting Canadians could then go to work for Omer.

So all in all, on that September morning, we had some 1,950 women and men ready to risk their lives in the service of humanity. We were proud of every one and grateful to have them poised for the strike, but we did not yet have enough to win. I knew that. Ben Freakley knew that. David Richards knew that. And back home, Mike Gauthier and Rick Hillier sure as hell knew that, because I had been screaming that

I first met Don Bolduc during my recce in theatre in 2005. He was on one of his countless tours commanding the 1st Battalion, Special Forces Group. We received a briefing from his team about the situation and I was impressed with their passion and knowledge. We were welcomed like any U.S. team would be, and he went through in detail what we would be facing. That information was important in order for us to gain a better understanding of what we were about to undertake. And Don's inclusive approach made it easy to generate a good working relationship with him. We next met when he rotated back into the south. I enjoyed working with Don and we established a good friendship. When Medusa kicked off we were under NATO of course, and it was our friendship that allowed us to figure out how we could work together to deal with the Taliban threat. We had frank conversations, and despite no formal command and control relationship we were two soldiers who were looking to find a solution to a problem. Don was typical of the OEF relationships we had fostered—and these were invaluable in obtaining critical support during Medusa. Don, a warrior who led by example, was critical in taking Sperwan Ghar and Siah Choy. Working with him was easy, because he understood the sense of urgency and acted decisively. His ad hoc TF 31—comprising three special forces ODAS, two 105mm howitzers and a company from the 2-87 (who we'd fought alongside earlier in the tour), along with many courageous members of the Afghan National Army— allowed us to defeat the Taliban on their own turf. I can still see Don's big smile and his overwhelm- ing enthusiasm to get into the fight. Don's unit did such a magnificent job that we wrote them up for the Commander-in-Chief Unit Commendation, which they received years later. I could not have been happier for these fine warriors.

truth to them for over a month. At least David had been honest with me. In a candid chat earlier I had asked him what further NATO support I could expect. His reply was: "Moral." I got what he meant.

Knowing I'd get nothing from NATO, I turned to U.S. Lieutenant Colonel Don Bolduc. Don was the commander of 1st Battalion, 3rd Special Forces Group, based like us at Kandahar Airfield. Reporting through Ben Freakley's 10th Mountain Division, Don's mission was to use his Green Beret special operations forces to conduct unconventional warfare in southern Afghanistan. Specifically, their job was to search for the enemy, find, fix and finish him, and attack him both kinetically and non-kinetically through the use of direct and indirect approaches. Just what I needed.

When I had arrived in Kandahar to do my reconnaissance in 2005, Don was already there. He rotated out for a time but was back in place when I took over RC South. His battalion excelled at their work, which included the kinds of construction and development projects we were doing. His special forces teams were experienced soldiers with backgrounds in engineering, civics and medicine. Much like ours, their mission might have them undertaking combat operations one day and providing humanitarian assistance, constructing roadways or working with local leaders to improve governance the next. He used to smile and say, "We're the Peace Corps with a bite."

When I was presented with the problem of force ratios in Operation Medusa, I went to Don and had a conversation as one professional to another. We had no formal relationship but we knew each other. I explained my situation and asked if he could help. He said, "Absolutely." With Ben Freakley's blessing he was able to provide me with a number of operational detachments of Green Berets who could take over an area of responsibility to the south, thus freeing Omer's battalion to push into Pashmul proper. Their specific role would be to act as a quick-reaction force, stopping Taliban ingress into Pashmul from south of the river around Sperwan and north of the river around Siah Choy. American special forces typically operate in small, elite groups, but in this instance Don Bolduc would have them all working together as a traditional force. But even then he would be too light on the ground. That problem was solved by Ben Freakley in the form of a seasoned U.S. infantry company. Known as the Catamounts (mountain cats) the 2nd Battalion, 87th Infantry Regiment had an ambitious mission: to deploy by air, sea or land, anywhere in the world, and to fight and win upon arrival. That's all they did and they did it with relish. As Ben Freakley put it, "Chris Stoner's 2nd Battalion, 87th Infantry Company had fought in Paktika, Kandahar, Helmand, Uruzgan and elsewhere. And those guys fought! There wasn't a week that went by in fifteen months that they weren't in a fight." They also knew the Canadians well, having fought with us in Sangin in July. They joined Don Bolduc's Green Berets and brought two 105mm howitzers with them for good measure. Together they became Task Force 31, and they would soon prove their reputation for quick reaction and ferocious combat ability. That gave us 250 more hard-fighting soldiers.

Supporting them all, we had air power. On the ground we had six British Harriers—vertical take-off fighters that could go from idle to wheels-up in under twelve minutes, and then be on top of any target in RC South in under two. And because we routinely had a dozen or so active TICs underway, we had fighters and bombers in the air every minute of the day and night. Most of these belonged to the United States Air Force, commanded in our region by Major General William Holland of Air Combat Command out of the USAF air base in Al Udeid, Qatar. The Americans had begun operating secretly out of Al Udeid in 2001, but by 2006 it was well known to all as a hub for logistics, command, and as a base for overseas U.S. air operations in places such as Iraq and Afghanistan. They controlled the allocation of Harriers, A-10s, F-16s—and, during Medusa, pushed in F-18s and marine Harriers to support us. It was astounding what we had at our disposal. F-16 Fighting Falcons (called Vipers by their pilots and crews because they look more like snakes than birds) could move around at Mach 1.2,

Aviation played a critical role in Regional Command South. Without helicopters, we could not have conducted medevac effectively or managed resupply and troop movement. Not having the use of attack helicopters to support our troops would have put us at a disadvantage. The U.S. under Operation Enduring Freedom (OEF) had a full aviation task force of approximately fifty helicopters, including Chinooks, Apaches and Blackhawks. They were amazing to work with and always there to support our operations. When needed, we could also obtain additional assets from Ben Freakley's 10th Mountain Division. After the handover to NATO/ISAF, this arrangement became much more diffi-cult to manage. Under OEF, I had direct tasking authority with the aviation task force. Under NATO, however, individual nations maintained command and tasking authority for aviation. In effect, the aviation support for RC South was reduced. The first tussle we had while transitioning to NATO came from our dogged insistence that we maintain a medevac capability. Under OEF, RC South had three dedicated medevac helicopters. These were deployed as necessary to ensure that wounded soldiers could be taken to a hospital in sixty minutes or less. NATO did not have any medevac capability. It was the Americans who left that in place for RC South after July 31. Without this intervention, we would have had to curtail our operations significantly.

climb to 50,000 feet in under a minute, and arrive on target to fire Vulcan six-barrel rotary cannons, Hydra rockets, Maverick and Harm missiles and AGM-158 air-to-surface missiles — or drop any kind of bomb needed to do the job. We had B-1 Lancer bombers (known as the Bone, from B-one) circling above with payloads of 56,000 kilos of ordnance each. The slow-moving B-52 Stratofortress bombers were also on station, with cannons, mines, missiles and bombs in a variety of configurations at the ready. Marine Harriers could be called on for additional support when vertical landing was necessary. In addition to air we had Task Force Knighthawk, a predominantly American aviation force comprising Chinooks, Blackhawks and Apache helicopters. Apaches, with their superior nose-mounted target acquisition and night vision equipment, also brought chain guns and Hellfire missiles into action while being able to hover, land and take off anywhere and under almost any condition, and our air cell could call on any of these at any time. Their pilots were smart, careful, energetic and dedicated pros who moved their platforms from one TIC to another with all the calm of Uber drivers. Perhaps more.

At last we had everything we needed. All in all we were now 2,200 men and women on a mission. We were ready to fight.

BOOK TWO

THE BATTLE

To better visualize the battle, refer to the
battle chart inside the back cover.

CHAPTER 14

STRIKE

Armoured dudes, we like to be comfortable, fat and happy.
Infantry dudes are different. They just want to go out and get messy.

MOTHER

September 2 was the day we began. Long before dawn, I took my position in the tactical operations room at our brigade head-quarters at Kandahar Airfield. We had a variety of forces in place, some on the ground, some in the air. Matthew Sprague's Charles Company and Mike Wright's A Company were ready to swing around Bazar-e-Panjwayi to secure the high features of M'sūm Ghar and Mar Ghar. A few days earlier, Geoff Abthorpe's Bravo Company had taken its position near Highway 1, ready to feint south at H-Hour while providing a northern screen throughout the battle.

At 0530, Charles and A companies moved out to M'sūm Ghar. From that vantage they would have an unobstructed view of objectives Rugby and Cricket, and dozens of Pashmul villages beyond. By 0600 they had arrived and found the high features unoccupied.

As the sun rose, the Canadians' view across the river was clear enough to see leaflets still cluttering the banks of the Arghandab. Intent on avoiding civilian casualties, we had airdropped warnings of our upcoming attack across the region. They could also see Taliban fighters at work setting up their defences. Easy, early targets. The LAVs of Charles Company rolled into line and began firing. Within minutes, at least ten of the enemy had been hit. Then all was quiet.

Omer Lavoie was now prepared to execute our plan, one he had rehearsed and refined in the rehearsal of concept (ROC) drill. No one liked the earlier start date, but today was going to be the day.

> This was to be NATO's first major combat operation, and at the time I was trying to make any ROC drills inclusive of the Afghan military police, local government if necessary, and the team at large. I would say that the ROC drill went okay. I did not see anything that caused me to believe they weren't ready to go, although I thought the objectives they picked should really be

Geoff Abthorpe was a gregarious, charismatic leader who always had a smile on his face. He was good at what he did—and he only got better as the tour went on. I would visit him in the field, and I greatly enjoyed our talks about tactics and the situation. I saw him develop into a highly capable combat commander.

broken down into smaller objectives, so that they could be pursued end-to-end more discretely.

BEN FREAKLEY

With the assets and enablers that Ben Freakley had freed up, our prospects were positive but we had to move quickly. Those resources wouldn't be ours forever. Greg Ivey's artillery battery set up camp 10 kilometres north of the battlespace, in an area that gave him enough room to position his M777s. From this artillery manoeuvre area (AMA), his guns began raining down fire on enemy positions in Rugby and

The LAV III was a home for many Canadian soldiers. They lived out of this remarkable vehicle for most of their tour. It provided them with the means to move around the region, and provided fire support with a mighty 25mm cannon along with two other machine guns. The optics on this vehicle gave us a tremendous advantage on the battlefield and it was critical to how we deployed during Operation Medusa. We used its protection, cross-country mobility and stand-off capability to the max when we attacked into the Pashmul area. It is not an overstatement to say that the LAV III saved lives. It was the best vehicle in theatre, and Canadians benefited hugely from the protection it offered. Its manufacturer, GDLS London, even modified this vehicle throughout our time in Afghanistan, improving the LAV's capabilities based on reports from soldiers in theatre.

Cricket, both of which were well within range of his howitzers. Apache attack helicopters wheeled around on station, moving as directed onto targets to fire their 30mm cannons, while Harriers and F-16s dropped 500-pound bombs and B-1 Lancers sent in precision-guided munitions from altitudes of 15,000 feet and above. Concussive waves rippled back across the river, and the sounds of the day could be heard hundreds of kilometres away. The battle was on.

South of M'sūm Ghar, Andy Lussier's Royal Canadian Dragoons sent back data on the movements of the enemy. But at 0930, they saw a horrific sight in the sky above them. A Royal Air Force Nimrod jet-engine surveillance aircraft drifted over their heads, spewing smoke and fire as it attempted to make Kandahar Airfield for an emergency landing. Originally a maritime patrol vessel, this particular Nimrod xv230 had been fitted with an electro-optical turret with the capability to transmit real-time video imagery to tactical commanders on the ground. We had been receiving a feed from the xv230 that morning. During a mid-air refuelling, a leak had occurred, allowing jet fuel to seep into the bomb bay where it was set on fire by either an electrical fault or the hot air from a heating pipe. The pilot reported the fire immediately, then dropped his aircraft from 23,000 to 3,000 feet in ninety seconds. An RAF Harrier scrambled to assist and was following the flaming aircraft as it passed over Task Force 31 and our ISTAR squadron. When just 40 kilometres shy of Kandahar Airfield, a first explosion tore one wing off and a second took the Nimrod apart. It crashed into the ground near the village of Chil Khor.

Andy's team immediately took off toward the site of the crash. Following the soldiers' code, they moved in to support with two priorities top-of-mind. They hoped to be able to tend to the injured if any survived. They also knew they had to reach the aircraft and its crew before the Taliban. A billowing pillar of smoke guided them as they neared, but as they entered the territory between Chil Khor and the neighbouring village of Fatehullah Qala, the twisting roads made the going uncertain. We had dispatched an Apache helicopter to the scene, and with their bird's-eye view its crew were able to guide the Dragoons to the exact spot. Tragically, there was nothing to recover. The fire, the blast and the crash had obliterated all twelve RAF personnel, one Royal Marine and one British soldier. Operation Medusa was under four hours old and we had fourteen dead.

Back at M'sūm Ghar the artillery barrage continued, while at brigade headquarters Omer and I were making decisions about the upcoming assault on Objective Rugby. I pressed for a night crossing. Omer had a number of reservations and stated his strong preference for a daylight advance. We compromised on an 0400 start for the next morning. In the interim, Omer had to decide where and how to cross the river. Looking over from M'sūm Ghar at the infamous white schoolhouse that had claimed four lives on August 3 when Ian Hope and his team rolled onto this exact spot, one thing was clear. Wherever we chose to cross the river, it would be wide. Even in September, when the Arghandab isn't at its peak flow, the distance from shore to shore can be a full kilometre, fully exposed. The crossing would likely be difficult. Even more so because, knowing we were coming, the Taliban would have mined all the expected crossings as they had the routes into Rugby from the north and east.

Engineers looked up and down the river for a tactically sound crossing. They knew that at least two platoons would head over at first, with engineers, clearance teams and troops from the Afghan National Army with their embedded American trainers. Key to all future efforts, a forward air controller would cross over with them to direct air support. Medics would be embedded too, to treat any wounded on the spot.

Ultimately, we made a tough but obvious decision. Charles Company would head from M'sūm Ghar directly across the river toward the objective. For a time, the conspicuous movement of Bravo Company in the north and a series of feints by Don Bolduc's Task Force 31 and Andy Lussier's ISTAR squadron in the south would keep the enemy guessing, so there would be at least some element of surprise. But that would end soon. The minute we began to ford the river in broad daylight, any doubt of our initial intent would be gone.

Artillery continued throughout the night, lighting up the sky in a fierce demonstration of firepower designed to confuse and overwhelm. Then, in the pre-dawn of Sunday, September 3, engineers headed down to the river to prepare for the crossing. They would have to breach both the river itself and a canal running parallel on the other side before our forces could move on the objective. It was near 0600 when the advance began, under cover of continued artillery and air support.

To our relief, the crossing was accomplished without incident. No IEDs. No rifle fire. No RPGs. No mortars. Mark Gasparotto's engineers breached each waterway at the best spot, and then two platoons from Charles Company made their way across river and canal and onto dry ground. There they established a beachhead with their LAVs, G-wagens, bulldozers and front-end loaders fanned out in a semicircle facing the known Taliban positions. So far no trouble, but by then the morning had become uncomfortably quiet.

The next phase of the advance would also depend on the engineers. A corrugated pattern of high berms had to be flattened and deep ditches filled to allow the vehicles to pass overland through the first wide field. By 0800 that was done. Dismounted infantry were sent out onto the flanks to ensure the outlying buildings were clear, while 7 Platoon rolled up towards the objective, its LAV IIIs leading and heavy equipment following behind. Within minutes the LAVs had reached the white schoolhouse, where they stopped short in line abreast. This was, they discovered, exactly what the Taliban commanders had anticipated.

Having shown remarkable discipline, the enemy had remained hidden and silent as we pulled right up below them. They then burst into action on three sides simultaneously, subjecting 7 Platoon to a furious, extended hailstorm of rifle and RPG fire, trapping the armoured vehicles where they had stopped and making any effective reaction virtually impossible.

One LAV took a round squarely, firing shrapnel from the turret ring deep down into the vehicle and killing Sergeant Shane Stachnik instantly. Then RPG and small-arms fire slammed into a G-wagen where Warrant Officer Richard Nolan sat in the front passenger seat. He was fatally struck on the first round. The driver of the now-smoking wagon signalled for help, which came swiftly as three soldiers from a nearby LAV dismounted and ran through continuous enemy fire to get to their stranded colleagues, giving whatever first aid they could and then carrying the wounded back through the gauntlet and into their armoured vehicle. Led by Sergeant Scott Fawcett, Corporal Jason Funnel and Private Michael O'Rourke then crossed that perilous distance four times in a row as they took their fellow soldiers to safety without a thought for their own.

As 7 Platoon coped with the ambush, 8 Platoon was still pressing up on the left flank in continuous firefights, clearing one building after another as they moved steadily forward. The enemy's knowledge of the layout of each building and connecting routes between them was superior, however. Even as 8 Platoon advanced, kicking doors, clearing houses and then moving on, the Taliban would reappear behind them having re-entered those buildings unseen. At the same time, units of the Afghan National Army were fighting up the right flank with impressive resolve, sometimes passing the men of Charles Company in their hurry to move on to the objective, and proving in the heat of battle that they too were fully committed to the fight.

By now everyone knew that the priority was to engage the enemy with enough force to free up the soldiers of 7 Platoon, who could then get their casualties back out of the firing line to be treated. Yet that withdrawal would have to be executed under constant enemy fire. When it began, one of the LAVs reversed out of the area and immediately hit a ditch where it ground to a halt, wheels spinning. Well within range, the Taliban poured fresh fire onto the vehicle, damaging but not piercing its armour on all sides. Another LAV pulled up to conduct a rescue. Its occupants jumped out to return fire, covering their comrades as they exited through the stranded vehicle's escape hatch and dove into the waiting, operational vehicle.

In constant communication, everyone back at brigade and battalion headquarters knew how desperate the situation had become. Our aircraft circled overhead, waiting to take out Taliban positions with high-powered explosives, but Charles Company was too close to the enemy for safe targeting. Even so, one fighter let loose a single bomb that landed among the LAVs and bounced right through the line. It never exploded.

Pressing their advantage, the Taliban escalated their rate of fire as the company attempted to recover its vehicles. While towing the damaged G-wagen back toward the river, the driver of the towing vehicle steered too close to a breach embankment, allowing the wagon to tumble into the ditch below. When another of the LAVs hit early in the fight was hitched and towed, its unconscious driver was jostled awake and was then able to regain positive control of the armoured vehicle and get it back into action.

Major Sprague decided to pull off the position and withdraw Charles Company to safety. He gave the order to set up a casualty collection point (CCP) where the wounded could be tended. At the same time, the remaining vehicles could be either recovered or destroyed where they lay to deny their use to the enemy.

The CCP is a doctrinal norm taught to all troops. During a fight, whenever critical casualties are incurred, the priority is to get the injured treated with first aid and evacuated. Each soldier is trained extensively in first aid and, when in battle, equipped with field dressings and tourniquets to treat their own injuries if able. They are also taught to treat others quickly and effectively. A certain number of soldiers in each section are also instructed in advanced tactical care of the wounded. In addition, each platoon has at least one or two medics, specifically trained in battlefield medical care. Once immediate care is given, the next step is to move the casualty away from the battle to behind the fighting, where further attention can be given and medical evacuation carried out.

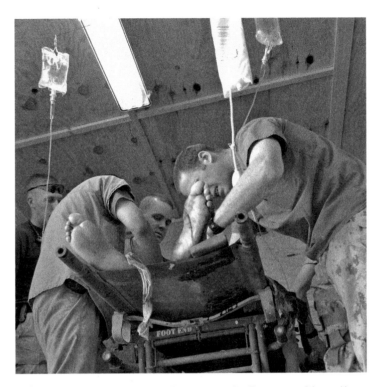

The medical support plan was one of those plans we spent an inordinate amount of time working on. We had four hospitals in RC South to attend to our wounded. The hospital success rate was well over 90 per cent. If it were not for these professionals, the consequences of the intense fighting would have been much more grave. Every time a soldier was wounded, the brigade sergeant major and I would go to the hospital to see what we could do and talk to them. Many times the media would be at the hospital door trying to get information. I would always walk in a back door to see the staff and the patients. This was about the troops, first and foremost, not a story. Visiting the hospital was part of my weekly routine, especially in quiet periods, which we didn't have many of. It was always great whenever I was able to sit down with the medical staff and hear their stories and tell them just how much we appreciated them. When they were not dealing with our wounded, they took care of Afghans. The injuries we saw were numerous—including oil burns and combat wounds. It was always difficult dealing with Afghan patients, because they would then go from getting the best medical treatment possible to returning to the Afghan medical system, which was less developed. The children were the hardest cases to deal with. We even asked for baby machinery, which perplexed Ottawa initially, until they understood the volume of work we were doing.

Every day I focused on where the soldiers were going to fight and how we'd be able to medevac them off the battlefield. Speed is critical. There's a proven concept called the golden hour. If you can get injured soldiers off the battlefield within an hour with competent medical care, they've got a 95 per cent chance of surviving their wounds. I was focused on that daily,

Medevac was another crucial element for us to plan and execute. No soldier ever went outside the wire without ensuring that we had a medevac helicopter within the golden hour. If that was not in the concept of operations (CONOP), I wouldn't approve it. Every man or woman had to know that they or their fellow soldiers would be taken care of in the event they were injured. This provided that little element of security that allowed everyone to focus on the task at hand. The medevac birds we had and their crews were heroes every day they flew. On board each aircraft was a specialized medic who would take over treatment of the casualty from the medic on the ground. When someone was wounded, we had medics right there. We also had other soldiers trained in advanced first aid. Every soldier also knew how to apply first aid to themselves. This system was critical to the overall operational effectiveness of our organization. Never have we put so much into the planning and execution of the medical system as we did during Afghanistan. My brigade surgeon, Lieutenant Colonel Jacques Ricard, was the best medical officer I have had the pleasure to work with. He and his team ensured we had the best medical support possible. Sadly, it was well used.

but I had limited medevac helicopters: only fifteen for the whole country; that was it. But I will say one thing: at no time ever was a soldier under my command, regardless of uniform or the flag they wore on that uniform, uncovered by a medical-evacuation helicopter, a network so they could talk and some form of fires. Not one day.

BEN FREAKLEY

It was Warrant Officer Frank Mellish who established the CPP that day, directing treatment of the casualties and arranging for evacuation. As part of the rescue mission, one of his soldiers was ordered to set off a white-smoke canister, and Greg Ivey's firebase on M'sūm Ghar was assured that all combatants west of that rising smoke were hostile. That information was greatly needed, because no one observing these events from back at the firebase could tell who was who. They then began to rain artillery onto the enemy, hoping to force them under cover while Charles Company got out.

After a firefight lasting more than seven long hours, Charles Company proceeded across and back to their initial battle position on M'sūm Ghar. In those first few hours of battle, they had suffered four fatalities and seen twelve wounded. Adam Day summed it up well in his account of Operation Medusa, published in *Legion Magazine* a year later:

They've been to a place beyond the normal world. They've seen their friends lying wounded on the ground, seen them die. And they've seen their own death: it was right there, in the rockets flying by—the end of everything. It's a place without illusions; a place where fear and courage are the same thing: live or die, you do your duty or you don't. It's a place from which any return is difficult.

Don't feel sorry for them, they don't want that. They are professional warriors and the first thing the men of Charles Company want you to know about the battle for Objective

Rugby is that they didn't lose. Not on the day. Not on the mission. The attack failed and it was bloody chaos. Yes. But the task force kicked a mighty amount of Taliban ass that day. The enemy were lined up and hidden, hundreds of them, firing from three sides. And the Canadians went forward, despite it all; they faced up and went into the guns, into the rockets, they attacked.

It was a tragic day, but we all knew what to do next. We would ready ourselves to go right back in.

CHAPTER 15

RESUPPLY

I'm easy to read. If you see a grin on my face, it means either that
I like something or that I don't like something.

MOTHER

O n the afternoon of September 3, the day we launched the
assault on Objective Rugby, Tim Bishop had walked into my
office and blurted out, "We're twenty minutes away from running out of 25 millimetre ammunition." I said something loud and
unpleasant followed by: "What changed from this morning's briefing?
It's just four hours later and we're down to nothing?" Tim told me that
(in Task Force Orion) the Patricia's battalion hadn't properly submitted
their ammunition expenditure reports, resulting in false assumptions on
our part about how much we had left. By the time they did submit and
our staff tallied the figures, it became obvious that our ammunition
depot was empty. John Conrad, in charge of logistics, walked into my
office at that moment. I asked the obvious question—"What the hell is
going on?"—to which he replied, "Oh, you've heard." I said, "Yeah, I've
heard." He said, "I've been trying to fix this for the past couple of days."
I said, "Really? Have you? That's terrific." (I did apologize to him later
for being sarcastic.)

We were indeed running out of ammunition, in part because
inept record-keeping had left us thinking we had more than we did,
and in part because the newly installed Task Force 3-06 had been firing
its weapons at more than twice the rate of the battalion they had

replaced. That was a shocker, especially because I got a daily briefing that included how many days of each class of ammunition we had on hand: x days of 25mm; y days of 155mm; z days of 7.62mm. That sort of thing. So there we were, about to face a deeply dug-in enemy armed to the teeth in what was going to be the fight of our lives, with twenty minutes' worth of ammunition left for the turret guns in our LAV IIIs, the vehicles that would be leading the charge. Fuck.

I contacted Mike Gauthier back in Ottawa: "I've got a problem in theatre. I'm running out of ammunition. Get me ammunition." My immediate issue was 25mm rounds for the LAVs, but then I found out we also had a shortage of 155mm ammunition. I told Omer to slow down the shooting until we sorted out the problem, and I made it clear we'd have to bring down the number of artillery shells fired in a day.

> I remember Fraser's message. It said: "25mm ammo low. 155 ammo getting low. 165 rounds fired yesterday, 116 rounds left." Canadian Armed Forces logisticians jumped in. Acting on advice from the army, they worked to figure out what ammo might be available in theatre and what could be accessed in Europe and so on.
>
> MIKE GAUTHIER

Ammunition had never been a problem before, but our firing rate in late August and early September had been off the charts, and certainly disproportional to its effect on the enemy. Ben Freakley had come to that conclusion himself already. When he visited around the time of the ROC drill, he had seen that the artillery effort was overly intense and largely ineffective—one more validation of our decision to put an end to it and get on with the fight earlier than originally planned.

The situation was critical. I would talk with Ottawa twice in the following three days saying we needed to fix this. There was no ammunition available anywhere in theatre, neither in Afghanistan nor Iraq. Not surprising. Everyone engaging an enemy in 2006 was firing the same ammunition. We had to expand our search around the world, and eventually found some in New Zealand.

I had learned that different battalions use ammunition differently, but I knew it would be unwise to draw rash conclusions. As commander of RC South I had watched only two Canadian battalions in action, and while one was standing off the other had been deliberately engaged in a phase of operations that required demonstration of firepower to the enemy.

Operational stocks were another issue. We were heading into battle with LAV IIIs, G-wagens, Bison, Coyotes and all manner of other vehicles. We were using everything we had in theatre. Whenever one of those got hit, we had nothing to replace it with. We had no system in place, no vehicles sitting in reserve. The only other vehicles we might call on were being used by other units in Canada to train the troops getting ready for the next rotation. It was the classic peacetime-army problem.

> These were the second- and third-order effects that arose after just the first few days of Medusa. As we looked at how things were going, it became an urgent necessity to align the thinking and actions at every level so our soldiers would be properly supported by their nation. As the fighting went ahead, the Prime Minister, Minister of Defence, Chief of the Defence Staff and Generals Richards and Freakley were all working to make a complex chain of command effective. And that was just for Medusa. At the same time, Dave Fraser had to look ahead to all the things coming next.
>
> MIKE GAUTHIER

I did think ahead. We were operating with a 360-degree view in a temporal reality where today, tomorrow and next month were all screaming for attention at once. As Omer was leading the local assault, I had to think about upcoming realities—including the start of Ramadan on September 23, the brigade RIP (relief in place) taking place on

November 1, and the imminent turnover of RC South to the Dutch, who were waiting in the wings. It was a surreal kind of pressure, where the immediate priorities of minute-by-minute combat had to be wisely managed even as decisions were made about things happening two, four and six weeks out.

It's testament to the quality of the RC South brigade headquarters staff that we had enough horsepower to focus on today without losing sight of the need to set the conditions for all the upcoming events. The trick was to keep focused on the immediate situation without overlooking the collective aim. I look back now in admiration at Chris Vernon, my British chief of staff, and Shane Schreiber, my assistant chief of operations. As everyone concentrated on the immediate fight — as they had to because it was dire — those two guys kept us on track.

So I did think ahead. But I never anticipated that what came next would be the worst day of my life.

CHAPTER 16

BLEED

The army trains you. Trains you great. Then they send you places to do and see horrible things and, after that, they throw at you, "You no longer meet universality of service standards."

That means you're done.

MOTHER

O n September 4 we were to begin again. As Omer later expressed it, the most important lesson from the day before was confirmation at the white schoolhouse of the adage that one can never make assumptions about the success of aerial bombardment against a low-tech enemy. Despite thousands of artillery shells, missiles and bombs dropped during the shaping phase of Medusa, the schoolhouse compound and surrounding buildings had proved resilient. The enemy had been able to maintain their positions using the vast network of indoor passages and underground tunnels that lay beneath the impenetrable walls of the structures in the area. The fighting would have to proceed piecemeal.

As we had anticipated, our intel confirmed the Taliban was now claiming a great victory against NATO. That they had repelled us. Listening to conversations between their commanders, we could tell that their fighters were feeling their power—or at least pretending to. But it was also clear they didn't know where we would come from next.

Our forces in the north and south made bold, early-morning feints to lead the enemy to assume we had changed our strategy. Whenever Taliban fighters came forward in response, we hit them with both artillery and air power. Apaches and A-10 Thunderbolts (known to their pilots as Warthogs) had been moving in and out of the designated kill box over Panjwayi, but ours wasn't their only mission. Aviation was supporting at least three efforts at the same time, orbiting between target runs in an area 40 kilometres north of us. From there in the still-dark morning, their pilots could clearly see the flashes of our artillery and the Apaches' exploding Hellfire missiles.

The airspace was busy. Sometimes too busy. Two mornings prior, we had put those same Apaches and A-10s into action, but not on their own. We also had an AC-130 gunship, two Hornets and an armed Predator on task, all of them coordinating attacks on a target barely three nautical miles wide. In between runs, they moved into a holding pattern, separated in theory in a stack of designated altitudes. But as three joint tactical air controllers (JTACs) were directing aircraft on three separate frequencies at the same time, an accident was likely.

Then A-10 pilot Captain David Raymond of the USAF advised our air support operations centre (ASOC) that he could coordinate the entire airspace from his aircraft while in our area. As a qualified forward air controller himself, Raymond could support all three JTACs, rack and stack the aircraft safely, and direct the simultaneous weapon employment of all the assets. Our ASOC granted his request. Raymond then had control of eight individual aircraft and could direct six tubes of our artillery. He requested we load and fire variable-time-fused rounds from our howitzers. They would explode in the air directly above and then onto our designated targets, making it possible for his pilots to direct their missiles and bombs with positive visual identification. Within minutes we had lit up, verified and taken out a major Taliban weapons cache. In his account of the night's work, Captain Raymond remarked on the unique nature of Medusa:

The notable thing about the sortie was being allowed to take control of the airborne stack, employing eight aircraft within a small target area and controlling artillery fire. Considering the asymmetric nature of the war, the minimal organic firepower the ground guys had, and the setup of the ATO [air tasking order], which usually only assigned two aircraft per geographic area, the weight of fire employed in that one kill box was monumental.

DAVID RAYMOND

But that was two days ago. The morning of September 4, our combat air support would not go as smoothly. In the pre-dawn, Omer was preparing to send his troops across the river once again. Most were up and moving at 0500, with the crossing scheduled for 0630. Charles Company and A Company readied themselves for a second strike, looking over at Objective Rugby which was then under heavy fire from the air. One of our forward air controllers (FACs) ordered two A-10s to wheel onto the white schoolhouse and drop 230-kilogram GBU-12 bombs on the compound; we wanted that hornet's nest reduced to rubble. At their altitude the A-10s had daylight on the horizon, making their night vision googles ineffective, but the ground around the target was still dark. The first A-10 moved in and dropped a bomb squarely on-target. Moments behind, his wingman flew directly at the smoke and fire and fired his 30mm cannon in a deadly strafing run. They conducted that sequence repeatedly, each time using the smoke as a guide to target.

But as Charles Company burned their morning's garbage in the dark, one of the A-10 pilots lost his situational awareness. After refuelling and returning to the kill box, he mistook the garbage fire south of the river for the fire at the target, locked his eyes on the smoke and wheeled in for another gun run. Had he verified the target on his heads-up display or targeting pod, he would have caught his mistake, but he did neither. Seeing what he took to be a group of Taliban warming themselves by the fire, he let go a short, deadly burst from his cannon into the Canadians. In mere seconds he killed Private Mark

Anthony Graham and wounded thirty other soldiers, including Charles Company's commander Matthew Sprague.

As the second A-10 closed in for the follow-up run, the forward operations officer on station jumped on the horn and called him off. Aware of the mistake and horrified by the result, the pilots of both A-10s ascended to altitude and entered a holding pattern as they regained their situational awareness. They then resumed their assault on Rugby.

On the ground, the situation was desperate. To mask the confusion following the incident, artillery fired a smoke canister onto the far shore. Perfectly placed, it expelled a long curtain of smoke blocking any Taliban view of the tragedy that Charles Company was suffering. Medevac support was ordered, and as the helicopter made its way toward the scene, a flare of purple smoke was ignited to signal the location. Once again, a pilot became disoriented. Mistaking the smoke screen on the north shore for the signal, the Chinook touched down right beside the enemy. Miraculously, the Taliban either didn't see or couldn't fire. The pilot realized his error, took off immediately and headed to the wounded.

This friendly fire incident illustrated the absolute chaos of the command-and-control system imposed on all of us. We had two completely separate chains of command operating at the same time: our own operations and special forces operations. Despite our efforts to de-conflict, airspace management was a recipe for disaster and the one thing I lost sleep over every night. The tragedy on September 4 proved it. At the time, the A-10s were supporting a special forces mission as well as our own, and confused their many targets with our troops on the ground. The ensuing investigation affirmed what all of us knew in theatre but had not been able to mitigate. We had all tried valiantly to manage this risk, but on this day we all lost.

Six months later, at a meeting of defence associates in Ottawa, Rick Hillier would underscore the gravity of those first two days of Operation Medusa, saying, "On that terrible weekend, they lost a company commander in action, lost a company sergeant major, lost one out of three platoon commanders, lost all three platoon warrant officers, one wounded, two killed, lost five section commanders out of nine and lost all of the sections' second-in-command master corporals—a total of forty-plus wounded and five killed in a forty-eight-hour period."

The incident had two immediate effects. First, it sickened us all. Second, it made us rethink the plan.

CHAPTER 17

ROUT

The boys asked me to stop reading out the intelligence reports before we went out into the rhubarb. Too upsetting. After that we just agreed it was going to be fucking Armageddon every day.

MOTHER

At the same time all these terrible events were happening at the river, Don Bolduc's Task Force 31 (TF 31) was living through its own hell south of M'sūm Ghar. When he had put his task force together at my request in late August, Don had included special forces teams and units of the Afghan National Army, over which he had placed Jared Hill in charge. Jared had arrived a year earlier to serve as Afghanistan assistant operations officer for the Combined Joint Special Operations Task Force. Now he was commanding Charlie Company of the 1st Battalion, 3rd Special Forces Group. Jared would soon face the challenges of command as he led his troops in some of the most ferocious combat activities of Operation Medusa.

Special forces operational detachment teams (ODAs) typically work in individual units. For Medusa, however, Jared would have three of these teams in the task force, with Captains Hodge, Bruce and Bradley leading ODAs 26, 36 and 31 respectively. These battle-hardened Green Berets would work together immediately before and during the operation to stop Taliban ingress into Panjwayi from the Red Desert and other points in the south. Soldiers of the Afghan National Army would be joining them for the fight. I asked Captain

Derek Prohar of the PPCLI to join them as my liaison officer. As special forces units communicate on frequencies different than those used by ground troops, Derek would take one of our radios and keep me informed throughout.

On August 29 TF 31 had headed for its assigned area of operations in the valley between the Red Desert and M'sūm Ghar, where we knew the Taliban were still active. Through phone chatter we had determined that Taliban commander Amir Sabar Mohammand had been mustering fighters in the general area to join the effort in Pashmul. To elude unwanted attention as they drove their eleven-vehicle convoy to the valley, the task force avoided roads and headed straight across the Red Desert in 50-degree Celsius heat. Based on intelligence gleaned en route both on the ground and over radio, it became clear to TF 31 that they were facing an enemy attack, one of significantly larger size than our earlier intelligence had led us to expect. When they exited the desert, they were immediately spotted as they had anticipated. Guessing that the attack would come soon, they positioned themselves on a ridge overlooking the valley and waited. As the sun set, they checked their gear, readied their weapons and dug in. Monitoring Taliban frequencies at dusk, they could hear the Taliban saying prayers. Then the radios went silent. Darkness fell.

The turret gunner in Jared's vehicle was the first to see them coming. One vehicle appeared. Then two. Then dozens. The Taliban were piloting their Hilux trucks to position their forces for attack around the battlefield. The task force's ground commander called for air support; we sent in a B-1 bomber, closely followed by an AC-130 gunship armed with 105mm and 40mm cannons. The AC-130 is a Hercules with an unpressurized cabin, its weaponry mounted down the port side of the fuselage. During an attack, the pilot will fly around the target in a slow pylon turn, making it possible to fire at the enemy for a sustained attack. It's a beast.

An ODA air controller called in the enemy's positions and, for safety, the position of our own troops. The AC-130 floated in, weapons ready to open fire on the Taliban—who were now taking flanking positions around the task force—if rules of engagement permitted. Under these restrictions, no aircraft has the authority to shoot unless an enemy weapon is visible, and the Taliban knew it. They hid their weapons immediately. Eventually, they simply moved off. The attack was over, for now.

Once again we had learned that the Taliban were becoming more sophisticated in their tactics, this time using our own rules to avoid slaughter from the air. The takeaway of this was that the Taliban were becoming significantly better organized in their ability to coordinate complex attacks. This was another new development.

The next day TF 31 waited in position. They were ready, but nothing came. As darkness fell again and no one approached, they concluded that the plan for an attack had been abandoned. The night was quiet. On August 31 they moved out, deliberately leaving fires burning so Taliban scouts would assume some of them were still in place. They then headed out of the valley and into the hills.

As they moved north, streams of locals passed them on the way out of the area. With our own information campaign and announcements by Governor Khalid, they all knew that a major showdown was coming. Even back then, one of my concerns was how quickly we could bring these people back to their homes once it was over. The disruption to their lives and livelihoods would be difficult.

This time the three ODAs split up, taking various positions on the mountains north of M'sūm Ghar, standing by to stop Taliban fighters from entering the area as their mission demanded, and ready to end the careers of any enemy fighters trying to flee the area once Medusa began. Jared Hill's Green Berets waited through September 1 and 2, listening to our aviation and Omer's artillery pound Panjwayi before the advance across the river. On September 2 they could feel the crash and explosion of the Nimrod not far behind them. On September 4 they listened to the news of the A-10 strafing of Charles

Company and heard that our main battalion was again going to have to pause and re-plan. They knew, as we did, that the operation was now in danger of failing.

As they were waiting, they could see the hill known as Sperwan Ghar to the south in an area we had designated as Objective Billiards. Though not even twenty metres high, it afforded any observer a 360-degree view of the surrounding valley and the battlespace north of the Arghandab. TF 31 figured that if they commanded the hill, they would have a vantage point from which to help target our air support. And we all knew that if the enemy were allowed to take the ground, it would severely restrict our future movement in the valley. We would be unable to manoeuvre when it was time to do so.

We hadn't paid as much attention to Sperwan Ghar as we had to Pashmul. We knew it had been a Soviet outpost in the eighties. A road circled up and around the hill to a summit into which the Russians had dug a circular depression, likely for a weapons battery. We were pretty sure the hill and the pit weren't being used for much now. At the foot of Sperwan Ghar stood a building complex with roads leading to its front and back walls. And that was it.

The plan to take the area was simple. Move in, sweep the roads, clear and take the buildings, then move up to the summit dealing with anyone in the way. Don Bolduc approved the plan and the teams rolled out, moving past villages, huts, ditches and abandoned vehicles, from which any Taliban snipers would have a clear shot. As Derek Prohar reported to me, nothing happened but, when they reached the Sperwan building complex, that all changed.

Just as Charles Company had experienced at the schoolhouse, all hell broke loose when the task force rolled up and the convoy was ambushed with small-arms and RPG fire from multiple directions. The enemy was entrenched, organized and fierce. All these Green Berets now knew they were somewhere of great strategic importance, and that the Taliban wasn't going to let it go easily. Once again Jared's team called for air support and were told they could have aviation on-site in twenty minutes. They guessed those twenty minutes were going to be brutal. They were right.

Out in the open, the vehicles of TF 31 were easy targets, and the enemy rained machine-gun fire and RPGs on them. But this was not the first time the ODAs had faced this kind of situation. They swung their vehicles around as screens, kept them all moving and returned fire with equal energy. At one point, they were engaged by a machine gun nest in one of the buildings, which upon inspection was obviously a mosque. Not a holy site that day, however, at least under our rules of engagement. The ODAs focused their firepower on the structure, eventually firing a round into the building from a portable, anti-tank AT-4. That silenced the occupants.

But the enemy around them seemed to be getting bolder, more determined. And at this rate of fire, the ODAs had already gone through half their ammunition. Predator feeds back at our operations centre were revealing that the Taliban were far more numerous than any of us expected, and we now knew this fight was going to be long and messy. Apache attack helicopters and A-10 Thunderbolts moved in and, while the risk of hitting our own soldiers was high because of their proximity, Jared's controllers were able at least to walk the nimble Apaches onto target with pinpoint accuracy. The firefight continued, with Taliban rising from the surrounding ditches to target the ODA vehicles, silenced in return by volleys of grenades. But the ODAs pressed on, even as the supporting aircraft had to leave to refuel. They cleared buildings, blew up weapons caches and killed Taliban fighters. But soon, within minutes, their ammunition would be gone. The order was given to break contact, and under full fire they withdrew. They drove south to a desert strip near a range of mountains and stopped to assess their damage. No one came after them.

The cost? One injury. No one killed. So far.

CHAPTER 18

SLAUGHTER

To this day, it's road kill that gets me. Fresh road kill. Too much like . . . you know. I hate that smell. I almost throw up every time I pass it.

MOTHER

G etting the wounded soldier evacuated was the first priority, and ammunition resupply was a close second. Both came fast. Intel was next. We needed to put a Predator drone overhead to give us an accurate picture of the evolving situation.

People today don't realize that when we went into Afghanistan, I had only one Predator line. I was a division commander, a two-star division commander, and I had only one Predator. Today every U.S. captain in theatre has a Predator he can direct. Back then, I had one. So it would work for Nick Nickleson in RC East or it would work for Dave Fraser in RC South, but it couldn't work for both.

BEN FREAKLEY

Today, that Predator was working for us. Controllers dispatched the unmanned aircraft to have a look at Sperwan Ghar and surrounds, and put a B-1 bomber on station to respond kinetically and immediately to whatever was found. That turned out to be fascinating. Within a kilometre of the hill there were other buildings and compounds in which they could now see significant activity. Toyota Hilux trucks were either moving toward or parked beside some key buildings, indicating that Taliban fighters had moved into position for the fight. As Derek Prohar reported to me, Jared Hill reviewed the Predator feed from the field, satisfied himself that there were no civilians at the site, then called in an airstrike. The B-1 moved in and obliged. From the Taliban chatter that followed, it became clear that many of their fighters and two of their senior commanders had been killed. The rest of the day would be quiet, but tomorrow TF 31 would have to go back in.

But, as it turned out, they did not go in the next day. Resupply Chinooks arrived throughout the day, escorted by Apaches. Both were fired on yet were able to deliver TF 31 its ammunition, fuel and food, and drop off their injured comrade who was now patched-up and ready to get back in the fight. With the final Chinook arriving only at mid-afternoon, the next attack on Sperwan Ghar would start close to dusk if it went ahead that same day. That would be tactically unsound given the Afghan National Army's limited night-vision capability and relative lack of experience in nighttime operations, two conditions that could expose TF 31 to potential fire by their own allies. Don Bolduc pressed them to go on, but left it to Jared to decide. He did. They would wait.

All eleven vehicles moved out just before dawn on September 5 toward Sperwan Ghar. They headed off-road to avoid mines and IEDs, and made it past the site of the previous ambush without incident. Then, as morning prayers blasted from the loudspeakers of nearby mosques, the Taliban emerged and began firing. After responding in kind, the task force dismounted and took cover behind the berms surrounding the hill. From here they could see a compound of seven buildings lower down the hill, and agreed they would have to clear those buildings and the schoolhouse at the bottom of Sperwan Ghar before fighting their way up to take the higher ground. In a fierce and extended firefight, they did exactly that, but they had to clear that schoolhouse twice. Just as Charles Company had experienced on its way to the white schoolhouse in Pashmul, the enemy was on its own terrain and knew all the hidden routes by which to re-enter cleared spaces and fire on coalition troops from the rear.

At several points in the fight TF 31 was fired upon from all sides, but they prevailed. Eventually they moved to higher ground and set up a .50 calibre machine gun to sweep back and forth across enemy positions, making it difficult for the Taliban to fire their weapons at the task force members at all. ANA riflemen took a nearby position spraying fire in a complementary arc from their tripod-mounted Kalashnikov machine gun. With the Taliban attack thus suppressed, the remaining ODAs charged toward the school to flush the enemy outside, where this time they would be downed by machine guns.

Once that was done, it was time to take the hill. Exiting the school, the assault force moved up the incline, spreading out as it progressed. When one ANA solider stepped on a mine, a reduction in tempo was ordered so a team could sweep for further hidden explosives on the way up. Their comrades fired on the enemy as cover. The going was dangerously slow, the combat long and exhausting, but the ascent was successful. They made the crest of the hill, targeted the last of the Taliban occupying the high feature, and stopped.

But not for long. The Taliban stormed right back at them from below. Looking down the hill, then confirming their observation using the Predator feed, TF 31 realized that enemy reinforcements were swarming into the schoolhouse and adjacent buildings, mustering their force ratio to attack the hill with greater effect. This was unexpected. Where were they coming from? After only a few minutes, even with air support, TF 31 was once again fighting for its life. The task force's own reinforcements arrived at the hill, but those vehicles were immediately attacked. One rolled over an IED, causing a number of casualties. Soon there were eight wounded soldiers at the casualty collection point and, with the seemingly growing number of heavily armed Taliban fighters, no Chinook could get anywhere near. The medevac had become a favoured target of the insurgents.

At length, the soldiers on the ground were able to direct tracer fire into key enemy positions, which gave the Apache pilots the guidance they needed to move in for decisive strikes. With many of the Taliban fighters under air attack, the Chinook then swept in to take away the wounded, even though still under fire itself.

Their wounded now heading to the hospital at Kandahar Airfield, the soldiers of TF 31 kept moving up the hill for what they knew would be a major attack from below. As they re-ascended, intelligence reported a considerable increase in enemy radio chatter, including a clear reference to a commander's palace. By taking Sperwan Ghar we had compromised a Taliban centre of strategic importance. As such, I had to declare that Sperwan Ghar would now become our main effort within Operation Medusa. While the task force held off the enemy, all available air power was shifted to the area. In the next few hours no fewer than twenty attack aircraft would participate in airstrikes at Sperwan Ghar, backed by a tanker to eliminate the need for aircraft to exit the area to refuel.

The strike was conducted by A-10s with three successive 1,000-pound bombs dropping on the buildings. These were followed up with gun runs, decimating the enemy positions. The enemy tried to move closer to deter the air support from making strikes, lest coalition planes hit their own men, but this did no good. The strikes continued and the Taliban fighters were badly compromised. After the A-10s left to refuel with the tanker, the Apaches arrived. They circled the area, flushing out and eliminating pockets of enemy fighters. Under the cover of the air strikes, the men on the ground dug into the school and found one room with useful intelligence about Taliban leadership that complemented and confirmed the rumours they had heard from passers-by when they emerged from the Red Desert. Even after the sun set, there was no let-up. A-10s and the AC-130 returned to continue strikes as the Chinooks doggedly kept up the vital inflow of resupplies. More than a hundred Taliban were killed that night alone.

The battle continued at this manic pace for two more days. On September 6 the task force could see at least two hundred Taliban moving across the river from the area of Siah Choy, the centre of enemy activity that we had defined as Objective Tennis. They crossed the Arghandab in their pickup trucks to attack as TF 31 rained machine-gun fire down the hill. A further assault was carried out against the schoolhouse, which was beginning to be the true focus of enemy interest. Clearly they wanted to reoccupy that space. What the hell was in there? Once again, intelligence reported numerous high-level Taliban leaders in the area, but we had known that before.

As the fighting continued over the next day, support for TF 31 continued to pour in. ISAF reinforcements arrived in earnest. Additional special forces operators joined the battle. Comanche Company from

We were blessed with an aviation task force led by the Americans. Comprising Chinooks, Blackhawks and Apache attack helicopters, medevac and combat search and rescue helos, this was my most flexible task force. High demand, low density meant that everyone wanted a piece of them. I never ceased to be amazed at how available they were and how willing they were to lean into any challenge. As the mission evolved, this task force expanded to include the Australians and Dutch. All contingents were superb, and critical to many operations.

the 10th Mountain Division moved in. More ANA soldiers moved down from areas closer to M'sūm Ghar. Bigger guns arrived. U.S. Navy Harriers from an aircraft carrier in the Indian Ocean appeared in the sky. And both Don Bolduc and Ben Freakley showed up in Ben's Blackhawk to inspect the battlefield. Weapons and equipment were in rough shape, torn by small-arms and rocket fire, shredded by shrapnel from mines and RPG shells. They found their soldiers battered, exhausted and some wounded, but all fully committed to whatever had to be done next.

With the pounding the Taliban was now taking, they shifted their tactics back from conventional to guerrilla combat, splintering into smaller groups that could move faster and hide more easily than a large force. They continued to cross the Arghandab in droves, rallying west of Sperwan near a hill called Zangabar Ghar. From there they drove east toward the hill and school building, which put them in the face of heavy task-force machine-gun fire. The Taliban death toll was growing fast. On one radio transmission, a commander admitted to having lost at least three hundred of his men . . . so far.

The flow of fighters into Zangabar Ghar had to be stopped. At noon on September 7, ODA 36 headed out to recce the location. It wasn't far, but when nearing the objective, rough terrain forced them to dismount and leave their vehicles behind as they made their way forward. The area was thick with tall vegetation and riddled with pathways cut by the Taliban through the brush. The recce team came upon a compound in which signs of life indicated that someone had just left. However, they weren't gone for long. Soon after, swarms of Taliban fighters were seen moving back through the irrigation ditches. ODA 36 engaged them.

Back at Sperwan Ghar, the rest of the task force could see clearly what was happening. Another wave of Taliban was crossing the Arghandab just north of Zangabar Ghar, then heading right for the compound in the brush. The ensuing firefight was furious and bloody. ODA 36 suffered numerous casualties, their team leader among them.

The rest of TF 31 and their ANA fellows fired down into the valley from Sperwan Ghar. Their view was excellent and their aim was true. As Hilux trucks with ten or more Taliban each plowed across the river, the task force unleashed a relentless barrage of firepower into the battlespace, killing anything that moved. To be blunt, it was slaughter. Next the Apaches moved in to clear the far side of the river in a devastating display of superior power. At the same time, an F-18 cleared a path out from the compound, pushing the Taliban far enough back so that ODA 36 could make a fast escape, which they did.

Supported from the air by experienced and savvy aviators, the soldiers of Task Force 31—Americans and Afghans together—had carried the day. After a week's unrelenting battle, the Taliban had been forced to abandon their positions on and around Sperwan Ghar, which to this day is a coalition forward operating base. Subsequent inspection of those buildings that the enemy had fought so hard to defend revealed that Sperwan Ghar had been not only a Taliban command post, but also the central training facility for all Taliban fighters in the region. We had wiped out their warfare school.

At a ceremony at Fort Bragg, North Carolina on May 23, 2012, these TF 31 members were honoured by Canada's Governor General and Commander-in-Chief with the presentation of the Commander-in-Chief Unit Commendation. This prestigious honour had been created in 2002 to recognize outstanding service by units of the Canadian Armed Forces that had been under direct fire in times of conflict. It is the highest level of award any military unit can receive from Canada, and only six such commendations had ever been awarded to Canadian Armed Forces units. The 1st Battalion, 3rd Special Forces Group was the first-ever, non-Canadian allied unit to be awarded this honour. The commendation read:

> During August and September 2006, the 1st Battalion, 3rd Special Forces Group (Airborne), United States Army, displayed extraordinary heroism and outstanding combat ability while

battling insurgents in support of a Canadian-led operation in Afghanistan. After completing their initial objectives, they willingly engaged a much larger force to secure the Canadian Battlegroup's flank and prevent the enemy from staging an effective counter-offensive. Outnumbered and facing a well-prepared enemy, they were relentless in their assault and eventually captured the position after days of intense fighting.

Many men had been wounded at Sperwan Ghar, among them Derek Prohar, the Canadian liaison to TF 31 who had kept me informed of the action I've just described. When I visited Sperwan Ghar soon after, I spoke with Derek and learned that he had been injured not once but three times in those seven days. The first was taking a shrapnel wound from an RPG shell. The second was being blown five feet in the air when his vehicle hit an IED. The third was having a bullet from an AK-47 hit him straight in the chest. Three times lucky.

The AK round was stopped by his body armour. I saw the hole in his uniform and the indentation in his armour myself. I was astounded to reflect that not once in all his radio reports had Derek ever bothered to mention himself.

CHAPTER 19

CONCLUDE

I have survivor's guilt, of course. We all do. My shrink—a little firecracker about this tall—says, "You fucking Army guys. (That's the way she talks.) You're all pressure cookers. Flip, flip, flip then BANG, you explode."

MOTHER

Rewind to September 4 at M'sūm Ghar. After friendly fire had stopped Charles Company on its way back into Objective Rugby, we had to rethink the plan. Both our strategy and configuration would have to change. We needed a fresh approach.

Charles Company was combat ineffective for the moment. They needed time to regroup. 1 RCR needed a new look at the situation, and we discussed our options. It was agreed that we would move Task Force 3-06 from the south up to Patrol Base Wilson where we would attack the enemy from the north. This had not been our chosen course of action at the beginning, because it would expose 1 RCR to the full strength of the enemy position and require them to fight through terrain and huts and buildings that favoured the defender. But after recent events we had no alternative.

Major Geoff Abthorpe and Bravo Company had already been sent via Highway 1 to take a position north of the Taliban defences. Their task was to patrol the edges of the battlespace, act as a northern screen and feint down onto objectives Cricket and Lacrosse to distract the enemy as Charles Company (in the original plan) went in to secure

Rugby. Engineers from 23 Field Squadron went with them to clear routes and create new roads as needed.

Bravo's first action was to work its way over to a sub-objective known as the "yellow school." The Taliban had been using the location to stage attacks on a section of the route between Kandahar Airfield and Patrol Base Wilson, a stretch we had all learned to call Ambush Alley. From there they were firing rockets and mortars onto Wilson itself. A host of Canadian reporters, many of whom filed their stories from Wilson's internet tent, had seen the impact of the attacks. Wilson was in rough shape.

At the yellow school, Bravo Company was immediately engaged. They returned fire in force, overwhelming the enemy within minutes. The feint had been a success, with the enemy drawn out and destroyed. The company then slowed down to maintain its holding pattern just above Objective Cricket, which stretched south from Highway 1. They patrolled this area, observing enemy activity from a distance and neutralizing any Taliban fighters who came within range.

Familiar only with the original plan and unaware of the rapidly evolving big picture, Abthorpe and his company were anticipating a day of enemy observation for both Bravo and Charles followed by three days of air bombardment before Charles moved across the Arghandab. But this had been accelerated. Convinced that our aerial attacks were having little strategic benefit and keenly aware of RC East's need to put those air assets in play, I moved the schedule up to assault Rugby immediately. When Charles Company then came under heavy fire at the schoolhouse, there was nothing Bravo Company could do in support except await further instructions. After the long firefight and Charles Company's withdrawal back across the river at M'sūm Ghar on September 3, we adjusted Bravo Company's task. Andy Lussier's ISTAR team spun up around the highway to join them and move together onto Objective Cricket, again hoping to make the enemy think we'd changed our plan of attack. On the morning of September 4, they were readying themselves to make that move when news reached them about the A-10 strafing.

Omer Lavoie directed Bravo to hold their northern position and asked the ISTAR squadron to return to the south until we could determine our next step. I told Omer to join me at brigade headquarters to reassess how to get across the river and achieve our objective. We looked at the overall situation and adjusted the plan to make our main attack from the north. For that to be successful, we'd have to switch things up and make the Taliban think we were now deploying our main force from the south.

Charles Company was depleted, but we needed them and they came through. While they had been through a brutal day of combat and a violent friendly fire accident, they were professionals and they stayed that way. I understand that many of the soldiers were later resentful of media coverage suggesting they were now in a pitiable state. The fact is, while a third of the company had indeed been wounded, two-thirds were prepped and ready to roll, which they did. We boosted their capabilities with additional snipers and air controllers, and joined them up with Major Lussier's ISTAR team to form the new Task Force Grizzly, which I asked Colonel Steve Williams to command.

Steve Williams had come to Afghanistan from Alaska, where he served as a National Guard brigade commander. He had deep operational experience both as a helicopter pilot and as a leader. In theatre he worked out of Kandahar as the U.S. National Command Element commander. Well aware of his leadership skill, operational experience and intimate relationship with the American chain of command, I asked him to serve also as my own deputy commander in RC South. He quickly became one of my go-to guys in the organization. Steve was an exceptional officer and a good person. Inventive, open-minded, charismatic and determined, he brought an aggressive can-do attitude to every challenge thrown his way. I needed that kind of warrior spirit on our team.

With Steve Williams at the helm of Task Force Grizzly, their role was now to hold the southern line—and, importantly, make the Taliban think they were a larger and more impressive force than they actually were. They had to be noisy. With that going on, we would then come down from the north. Hard.

I would spend as much time as I could in the field during Medusa with the commanders on the ground. Steve Williams's (in the foreground right) understanding of the overall plan, coupled with his grit and determination, made him a critical part of the overall combat force. He was a good tactician and his observations and recommendations were always insightful and helpful to me. On the far right stands my formation sergeant major, Mike MacDonald. A quiet man who could speak volumes with few words, when Mike spoke we all listened. He was a keen athlete and great gunner. He was my fire team partner and someone I trusted without reservation. He was my sounding board, and the one person who knew me better than anyone else in the formation. We were a tight command team; like a married couple, really. Everywhere we went, we would talk to different people and then compare notes. I could not have completed this mission without him being there. He was my rock.

Knowing that we would now be moving through dozens of the near-impenetrable grape-drying huts on our way south, I was concerned that we did not have the right equipment. As we had learned painfully at the white schoolhouse, many days of punishment by aerial bombardment would not obliterate the enemy. I figured we needed a weapon that could move with the soldiers on the ground and take out the walls of any grape hut we came upon. I needed tanks.

To be precise, I wanted the standoff capability of a tank with a 105mm or 120mm gun. Tanks have better range and produce better effects than artillery, in that a tank shell will go through mud walls that are as strong as concrete, won't cause the damage a 2,000-pound bomb does, and will stop the people inside who are shooting at you. The other benefit of using a tank is that it scares the crap out of people. It's a big lethal force with huge psychological impact. I wouldn't have ever thought about using tanks at the beginning of our tour, but when strategic and operational conditions began changing so quickly during Operation Medusa, I knew that tanks would deliver the tactical effect we needed.

On September 6, I wrote to Rick Hillier asking for six tanks. He wrote back saying I hadn't asked for enough. If we needed tanks at all we needed at least ten. He would send half a squadron of Leopard C2s. These German-built units had long been the tank of choice for Canada's army. With heavy armour, each one weighs over 50 tonnes, and even so can travel over 65 kilometres per hour. But at the time that I asked for the tanks, the Royal Canadian Armoured Corps was actually disposing of tanks from the Canadian inventory. The tanks were being systematically decommissioned, but I made the request anyway.

When he had been commander of the army, Rick Hillier had said he didn't need tanks. But then the game changed. The game changer was Afghanistan. Operation Medusa saved tanks for the army.

MIKE GAUTHIER

Throughout the tour, we adjusted our tactics and techniques to meet the ever-changing Taliban and the evolving conditions on the ground. When we arrived, the risk tolerance was quite large, but it diminished over time. This was particularly true after the switch over to NATO. I attribute this in large part to their operational tempo, which was very different from RC East. The 10th Mountain Division under Ben Freakley operated at a much higher tempo, and combat was an hourly occurrence. Regardless, as the mission progressed and the Taliban nestled into villages near civilians, the use of GPS-guided bombs and hellfire missiles caused too much damage. We found we needed more accuracy to deal with the enemy, and the 25mm cannon on the LAVs, great as they were, did not have the range or punch we required. We did a detailed analysis and came up with a solution—the tank! Why? It had range and mitigated the collateral damage, and it had the psychological effect we were looking for. We always told the troops to overmatch the enemy in every engagement. Tanks would provide us with the range, optics and punch necessary to keep doing just that. Using a tank also demonstrated our resolve to the enemy and Afghans alike. It would be clear we were here to do business. When we wrote the letter requesting tanks to the Chief of the Defence Staff, Rick Hillier, we thought that it might raise a few eyebrows. Back home, tanks were being taken out of the inventory and put up as monuments. The reply back from Rick was swift: **request approved but you didn't ask for enough; more coming**. This was a key boost to our capabilities. The tank needed to be used judiciously, because it certainly would have an escalating effect on the IED threat. Over time, they became so commonplace that the IED threat grew tremendously because of Taliban's desire to kill a tank. Nothing comes without a cost.

When I spoke with the guys back at the [Lord Strathcona's Horse] regiment, they said it was "All hands on deck. We just got warned we're coming in with tanks." "Really?" I said. "Whoa, never saw that coming." It was up to them to get the Leopards up and running. Some of them were already mothballed, and others had to be torn off monuments!

MOTHER

Captain Edward Stewart, our forward public affairs officer, later noted in his summary of Operation Medusa that "a persistent rumour began to circulate that a squadron of Leopard C2 tanks from Canada would shortly be joining the fray. Although they would arrive in theatre too late to affect the battle, it was noted by many that this was the first time in their memory that a crazy rumour turned out to be true."

In the end they did arrive too late for the battle, but they were put to constant use in theatre anyway.

Even without tanks, Bravo Company's role was front and centre. Where they had once been the anvil, they were now the hammer. They would be joined by Task Force Mohawk, a veteran force from Ben Freakley's 10th Mountain Division which had swung in from Zabul province to help us get the job done. We now had Bravo Company and Mohawk to push down from the north; Task Force Grizzly appearing to attack into Rugby from M'sūm Ghar; and Task Force 31 routing the enemy out of Sperwan Ghar, then acting as a southern screen.

In preparation for the push, Bravo Company needed to choose its route from Highway 1 down toward Rugby. Every option would require cutting through classic and intensely inconvenient Panjwayi features such as *wadis*, marijuana fields, irrigation ditches and the infamous grape huts. They were ready to move out to make enemy contact, but early on it came to meet them. While the Canadians were restocking for the upcoming journey, four soldiers of Bravo Company were targeted by a group of Taliban attempting to flank their position. The enemy hit one of the LAVs with RPGs and 82mm recoilless-rifle fire. Once that attack was repelled, Bravo moved out.

They established a pattern of nighttime reconnaissance to plot the next day's chosen course. Come morning, artillery and air support would flatten the area, and the waiting company would move through the cleared space onto the next objective, which they would occupy and secure.

They met at first with minimal resistance, particularly given the sideshows happening to the south and southeast with Task Force Grizzly and Task Force 31. With hindsight we know that we had forced the Taliban to make Sperwan Ghar their main effort, so fighters who might otherwise be resisting Bravo Company's descent had been dispatched south to cross the Arghandab and reinforce their troops there.

While Bravo Company led the push south, it was a shared effort with A Company and Mohawk company, all of whom engaged in a classic manoeuvre known as a "forward passage of lines." This leapfrogging tactic allows units, in successive turns, to move with cover through one another's area as they pursue the next objective. Over the next several days, the three companies followed that progression through the heart of occupied Taliban territory all the way through to Objective Rugby.

The Taliban was employing Second World War tactics during the advance. Their formations and behaviours became almost predictable as the battlegroup progressed. In this regard, the fighting had indeed turned to conventional warfare as predicted. And as we had hoped, the combination of artillery, air support and constant fire from our advancing soldiers proved a critical disrupter to the Taliban. They could never once get out from under it to advance.

Objective Cricket was finally taken over a period of two days. Bravo Company took the northern half on September 10, followed by the U.S. Mohawk team taking the southern half on September 11. The same day, I had a brief radio conversation with Steve Williams of Task Force Grizzly who was still in position at M'süm Ghar. Steve and his men had been itching to move across the river and get into the action but were standing by for my order. As they waited they had been firing everything they had at the enemy, including heavy-metal music cranked to eleven on the dial. Under Ben Freakley's tutelage, Steve had become a warrior who would use any means to confuse and dominate the enemy.

> I'm a big believer in a term called *constant pressure*. When you
> go to fight an enemy, you have to overwhelm that enemy with

Here we see my deputy commander Colonel Steve Williams and me walking with the herd during Medusa. Steve was a National Guard brigade commander who was the U.S. national command element commander in Kandahar. When I met Steve, I immediately liked his professionalism, character and warrior spirit. We were on the same page. He spoke truth to power and I appreciated his straight talking. When we needed more combat power following the tragic friendly fire incident on September 4, I asked Steve if he could deploy. He said yes immediately and Task Force Grizzly was created soon thereafter. Steve led the remnants of Charles Company and other assets we had given him to create the deception that 1 RCR was still in location while we moved Omer Lavoie's team up north. During the final push onto Objective Rugby, Steve didn't waste any time in crossing the Arghandab River and taking the eastern portion of Rugby. Steve was the right leader to be in charge of Charles Company after their tragic few days, and led them to take the objective that had cost them so much. He was one of my best leaders during Operation Medusa.

constant pressure using every capability you have: psychological warfare, use of fires, artillery and joint air power, and direct fire. You must confront the enemy visually so that he sees and knows you intend to win. If you've ever watched the movie *Zulu*, you will have seen the sequence when the British, who are all down at the station, look up and see thousands of Zulu warriors coming up on them. As they surround the British, the Zulus are all chanting in unison. That's constant pressure.

BEN FREAKLEY

Task Force Grizzly hadn't been together long enough to master a chant, but the interminable blasting of their dissonant rock music had achieved much the same effect. When I heard that Steve had been waiting for my order, I replied that I had been waiting for him to move. I don't think he even signed off before Task Force Grizzly took off across the Arghandab. There they met with only a manageable degree of resistance so, with support from the Afghan National Police, they made the far shore and secured a position east of the white school-house in the centre of Objective Rugby.

Rugby was still our main objective, and we now had everything in place to complete it. We took Objective Lacrosse on September 12. We then needed a coordinated final push at an accelerated tempo. In stark contrast to the events of September 3, the enemy was now weakened, offering minimal resistance in some areas and none at all in others. As the battlegroup closed in, all units systematically cleared the objective, one room of one structure at a time. They stripped the hinges off the doors of each building, tossed grenades into hidden spaces, then entered firing.

By then, Don Bolduc's Task Force 31 had left Sperwan Ghar to cross the river and tackle the enemy force in Siah Choy, from which so many Taliban reinforcements had poured across the river to defend the Taliban training centre. But they found Siah Choy empty. Three scenarios were possible. First, we had killed the entire Siah Choy contingent when they were on the other side of the river. Second, they were heading back into Pashmul to fight us there. Third, they had exited the area by moving south, back into the desert. If so, our British forces would take care of them.

In the end it was the soldiers of Charles Company who moved against the white schoolhouse itself, fitting retribution for the opening ambush that had forced them to withdraw. When the battlespace was at last cleared of Taliban, they walked through the scene, all quiet now, to learn what they could about the enemy's tactical plan.

Two revelations emerged. First, an analysis of the enemy's fortifications proved that the Taliban had indeed positioned their stronghold to repel an attack from the south. The way they had reinforced their bunkers, constructed their trench systems and camouflaged their locations all showed that they had anticipated our force from that direction. Our deliberate avoidance of that route had served us well after all. Second, inspection of the subterranean spaces and tunnels in the vicinity of the complex confirmed, as we had concluded, that two or three more days of aerial bombardment would have accomplished little or nothing. The Taliban had buried themselves deep in the ground and were prepared and able to wait us out. No matter when we had arrived, they would have been there to meet us.

For the next few days we pushed further westward. When we arrived without meeting any resistance at the 24 Easting, a line of longitude we had defined as the logical outer limit of our battlespace, we concluded that the enemy had fled. That was September 16. We learned later that some 400 Taliban had moved west out of Kandahar Province through Helmand into Farah, Afghanistan's western province bordering Iran.

The following day, General David Richards asked the question, "Are we done?" I returned, "We're now at the 24 Easting, and our info ops and intelligence teams report that the enemy has run away from us out of the area. Therefore, yes, I'd say we're done." Our Commander ISAF was then able to declare Operation Medusa over.

My dominant thought was one of relief. We hadn't lost.

The soldiers in Afghanistan were the most important asset we had. They had been sent there by politicians, but it was their belief in what they were doing that made a difference to the effects on the ground. Soldiers (and when I say that I also include sailors, airmen and airwomen) did more than the average person would think. In addition to their military tasks, they were teachers and communicators providing assistance to the Afghan people—and generally demonstrated all that was good in each of us. I have never been more proud than I was watching each soldier do what he or she knew was right. Inherent in all of them was courage, determination and an admirable sense of duty. But their greatest trait was their humility. People back home in Canada and other nations alike would write to soldiers sending messages of thanks, encouragement and prayers. The soldiers in turn would be embarrassed to a degree with all the attention. They were all doing what they believed in. I always took time to go out of headquarters to listen to the soldiers and ask them what was happening. There was no better measure of the metrics of a mission than to ask a soldier what he or she thought. They were the front lines and they would tell you, without varnish, how things were really going. Throughout history, missions have been built on the backs of soldiers. Technology has improved but the most important thing we have is still our people.

CHAPTER 20

TALLY

I always worried about the safety of my people. It's why I'm such
a mess to this day.

MOTHER

W as it worth it? That question has been posed by everyone who
has ever served in Afghanistan. For those of us who were there
in September 2006, the question is specifically: *Was
Operation Medusa worth the cost in effort and sacrifice of human life?*
There is no simple answer, yet many people have come to strong opinions.
My own view was from the commander's seat, where over time I formed
my understanding of why we went in, what it cost us and what we achieved.

Let's begin with some bleak statistics. During the years from 2001
to 2017, more than 50,000 Taliban were killed, most of those being
Afghan men and boys forced into service by either poverty or threat
of violence against their families. In that same time, more than 38,000
members of the Afghanistan National Army, Afghanistan National
Police and other arms of the country's security forces were killed, proving
that the greatest sacrifice in this campaign was made by the Afghans
themselves. Among the U.S. and coalition forces, some 3,500 men and
women died, including 159 Canadian soldiers and 3 Canadian civilians.
At least 2,000 other civilian contractors also perished, even as they
worked to repair the damage to local infrastructure caused by the war.
Perhaps most tragic, more than 30,000 civilian men, women and children were killed during the struggle. During Operation Medusa, from

August 19 to September 17, 2006, six Canadian and twelve British personnel died and more than fifty were wounded. And while the true number of Taliban deaths in that time will never be known, a reasonable estimate would put their toll between 1,000 and 1,500.

There are positive statistics as well. Omar Samad, Afghan ambassador to Canada, reported in 2006 that thanks to the stabilizing effects

The Leopard tank was the last thing we thought we would need in a counter-insurgency. This was supposed to be about hearts and minds, engaging the people, and fighting the Taliban when necessary. Tanks were designed to deal with other tanks or armoured vehicles. There were none in Afghanistan that worked, and those that did sat in hangars. When we were faced with increased restrictions regarding collateral damage, the weapons we had at our disposal—including GPS-guided bombs—created too much of an undesired effect. Our analysis led us to the need for tanks, which had more precision and optics to limit their lethal effects. The speed with which the tanks were introduced attests to the will in Ottawa to support the troops, and their understanding of just how important this fight was. I don't think Canada could have generated this effect as quickly if we had asked for them earlier in the mission. It attests to just how much the whole-of-government team had progressed. In theatre, the other coalition partners were surprised at just how fast our team back home in Canada was responding to our needs to make sure we could succeed in our mission.

of coalition efforts, five million children had gone back to school. Three million displaced Afghans had returned to the country. The nation adopted a democratic constitution for the first time in its history and, for the ensuing presidential elections, the voter turnout was a record 80 per cent. By the end of 2006 there were sixty-eight women parliamentarians in office. More than 130 publications, television and radio stations had formed a free press. More than 10,000 weapons had been gathered and either destroyed or stored. And with the eventual input of Canada's CIDA, and DFAIT and DND—the three Ds of development, diplomacy and defence—a vast number of programs had helped rebuild the economy of the nation, including savings and micro-loan services to 140,000 clients, of whom almost 90 per cent were women. Had we built a nation? No. But we had helped a nation take many steps to rebuilding itself. Had we lost the fight during Operation Medusa, none of those steps would have been taken. As Colonel Brian MacDonald wrote in TAO *Magazine* in 2006:

> With our OEF and NATO partners, Canadians have helped Afghans and the Afghanistan government to develop a new constitution, conduct successful presidential and legislative elections, get more than one million girls enrolled in school, begin reforms in defence, justice and finance, and begin the reintegration of nearly three million Afghan refugees. And the role of the Canadian Armed Forces in Afghanistan is to protect that work, by the use of deadly force if necessary, against those who would seek to kill the civilians, the Afghan[s], the Canadians and our other partners, who would destroy all that we have achieved, and who would turn back the clock to the oppression of earlier regimes. That is why the Canadian Armed Forces are there.

An important upshot of our time in Afghanistan was the depth and volume of what we learned. We had gone over to assist, so our Canadian mission was straightforward, at least on paper. Task Force

Afghanistan would conduct whole-of-government, discrete yet synchronized operations across the full spectrum of conflict in order to support Afghanistan's effort to create a secure, democratic and self-sustaining nation state.

We had named our task force Aegis after the shield that protected the Greek gods Zeus and Athena. Bearing the image of a Gorgon head with her hair of live snakes, the Aegis was a source of great power, knowledge and well-being to those who carried it into battle. We figured we could use those. We would go in as a combined task force composed of elements from the army, air force, navy and special forces.

In the subsequent melding of our Canadian mission with ISAF's in RC South, we evolved a more nuanced mission statement that all contributing nations eventually signed onto:

> CTF AEGIS undertakes full spectrum operations in order to enable GOA [Government of Afghanistan] efforts to defeat the adversary forces and create a secure, democratic and self-sustaining Afghan nation state.

We went as a team of teams, with military, diplomatic and development experts. As part of the thirty-seven nations contributing troops, we joined a larger mission to conduct military operations in our assigned area, making it possible for the Government of Afghanistan to establish and maintain a safe, secure environment with full engagement of the Afghan national security forces. While no one questioned the merit of our objective, how it would be executed would be confused and frustrated by thirty-seven national interpretations, thirty-seven approaches to military training and operations, thirty-seven systems of national resourcing and thirty-seven ever-changing lists of national restraints and constraints both stated and unstated. Competing opinions about what we should be doing and how it should be done would complicate the lives of each man and woman who joined the tour, as would the actions of the Taliban.

Coalition operations are never pretty. To succeed they require reasonable give and take negotiated through tremendous amounts of dialogue. The uneven distribution of resources among coalition partners and the willingness (or lack thereof) to share capabilities needed by others made figuring out how to deliver any one desired effect even more complex. Under OEF we had seen the United States provide a reasonable balance of support across each province and contingent, but under ISAF each province was the responsibility of one nation alone tasked with coordinating all activities related to security, diplomacy and development. With such a broad mandate, nations tended to be less willing to share assets such as aircraft, vehicles and even their own troops. That made conducting regional operations painful. During Operation Medusa many nations simply would not show up to fight at all. Planning was agony. Even when the operation was only days away, we weren't certain who would support us at H-Hour. Many of the caveats exercised had never been put down in writing; instead they were decisions of the moment, presumably made in national capitals by people with no idea of the stakes. When members of the North Atlantic Council visited us (inconveniently) during the fight, I relayed the severe impediment that these national constraints had put in the way of our mission.

NATO's mission in Afghanistan had been touted as a coalition of the willing; however, in practice we all found it to be a coalition of arbitrary limitation. This foot-dragging was never the fault of the men and women in theatre; they were trained, motivated and willing to fight. It was the aversion their governments had to all political risk that forced most of their soldiers to watch Operation Medusa from the sidelines. This left the Canadians to shoulder the burden of the fight, with the Americans, Dutch, British and Danes moving in to make this impossible coalition work.

Operation Medusa was but one of many hundreds of operations under Operation Enduring Freedom and the ISAF coalition. Yet it was the biggest fight either OEF or ISAF undertook there, with unique pressures and expectations. Among these were the constantly changing timeframes within which any action could be executed and, ultimately, judged to be effective or not. We wouldn't know for days or weeks whether a specific military effort had been successful. The tangible benefit of any development project couldn't be known for years. And whether our all-important capacity-building efforts have really made a difference can be judged only by future generations.

The chief impediment to our progress, of course, was the state of the nation. When we arrived in Afghanistan, its democratic government was only five years old. It was born in 2001 and—like any five-year old—was energetic and immature, despite a depth of culture that stretches back into ancient history. In hindsight our expectations in Afghanistan were wildly optimistic and certainly unrealistic, especially the timeframes within which we believed we'd see progress. A major obstacle to our understanding was our own lack of knowledge and understanding of the role of tribal culture and politics in Afghan society. Afghanistan does not exist in the minds of most Afghans; to them, their tribe is everything. Most locals do not travel outside of their tribal surrounds and are very much tied to the village of their birth. In Afghanistan today, as in Pakistan, the authority to govern comes from a nuanced interplay between an elected federal parliament and the varied systems embraced by the individual tribes whose members make up the population. And while the tribal elders have the moral authority of the people, the elected Afghan leaders control the resources the tribal elders need. We worked hard to bring both groups together and establish a means for them to work jointly for the benefit both of the tribes and of Afghanistan as a country. Early on we partnered with leaders such as Asadullah Khalid. We put their weaknesses aside; they were the people we had to work with. When I think back on them now, my chief memory is simply how courageous they had to be just to survive. Most did their best, by and large.

Much of our work took longer and was more complicated than could be explained by the embedded media. In most cases those reporters, as hard as they worked and as eager as they were to state the facts, did not report the bulk of what we were doing vis-à-vis development and capacity-building. Those topics were boring, alas. We were routinely disappointed that the headlines back in Canada and around the world were always about combat, as in the long run it was what we were building, not destroying, that mattered most to us.

Within our own coalition camps we had to learn how to work together as whole-of-government teams. Coming as we all did from nations where interdepartmental cooperation is expected and routine, one would think such collaboration would be straightforward even in the field. Wrong. Here's a surprise: the complexity of joint action between governmental agencies from multiple countries working on foreign soil to serve populations whose languages they don't understand on behalf of a nascent democracy at war with a terrorist insurgency using the proceeds of illegal drug production to acquire weapons from neighbouring states did not turn out to be as easy as our deputy ministers assumed. Every nation represented, despite all the chest-thumping about how great their campaign plans were, had to stumble for a while, and then invent a system with defined procedures by which their own institutions could work together. Great credit must go to the men and women on the ground who made it work, our own Simon Hetherington, Pamela Isfeld and Christina Green among them. They and their counterparts in other coalition nations resolutely pushed back up their respective chains of command for adjustments to enable them to get more done on the ground. In Ottawa key leaders were onboard; however, bureaucracies and procedures hamstrung everyone. Over time these issues were ameliorated, but the early rotations — including ours — had to endure the pain of building a concept of national operations from scratch.

The Canadian Army's focus on battlegroup operations had worked well for decades, but Afghanistan changed the rules of the game. In the current operational environment, brigades must now be the lowest-level organizations to manage the resources needed for mission success. Intelligence, air space planning and coordination, Special Forces planning, logistics, medical planning and evacuation, whole-of-government collaboration, inter-agency coordination and coalition dynamics are just a few of the many higher-level activities that brigades can handle effectively, while they would overwhelm lower organizations. Afghanistan changed the paradigm, and the paradigm continues to evolve with every new threat.

On the military side, operating in combat once again illuminated some weaknesses in our design. Our leave policies posed a significant problem because, well, people went home on leave. Units had to manage more risk than planned for, because they were never fighting with full strength. We had understood this going in, of course. The real difficulty arose when NATO made assumptions about the combat-effective strength of our units based on their paper strength alone. Rotation lengths were another issue. Canada chose a six-month length of tour for fighting units and a ten-to-twelve-month tour for headquarters staff. This was a national decision that considered the effectiveness, health and morale of our soldiers in the field. The rationale was sound, but not everyone did as we did. Americans, for instance, kept their troops in theatre for twelve months, and they chose to increase that duration based on operational necessity twice during our own rotation. They found that soldiers who stayed longer were smarter, bolder, safer and more effective. Each tour comes in, picks up the rope from the previous tour, and pulls it until they hand it over to the next rotation. Rick Hillier was clear at the beginning that he wanted all of us to get away from thinking that each rotation was unique. Our mission needed continuity. We had to focus more on providing hope and opportunity to Afghans, and less on our own concerns. I don't believe we ever achieved his intent in the duration of Canada's involvement in Afghanistan.

Both OEF and ISAF adopted a philosophy called "Afghan lead." It was the right approach. We went out on most (our aim was all) operations with an Afghan unit alongside us. When we went into a building, the aim was to have Afghans go in first. This sent a message to their people that they were not only part of the operation but were leading it. In reality, we did the bulk of the planning, although we did collaborate with the Afghan leadership as much as possible and within security constraints. The Afghan lead concept was not effective initially because of the lack of skill among the Afghans. When I went back for later visits, however, I saw demonstrable improvement with the Afghans planning, rehearsing and conducting operations on their own.

Back in 2006, the expectations we had about how much and how fast the Afghans could deliver were unrealistic. Much criticism has been levelled at Afghan leaders and organizations. Certainly there were many who were corrupt and incompetent, but we quickly learned who we could work with and who we should not, and things did get better as time went along. The situation evolved from us complaining "if only they were doing something" to exploring how they could get things done better. When I first met Governor Khalid, in the middle of a conversation he might answer his cell phone and race out of our meeting, pick up his AK-47 and rush to the scene of a firefight. Not what you would expect from one of our provincial leaders in Canada. With our guidance, Khalid began to work instead with his own chain of command, relying on his security force to brief him on plans and actions when events occurred. That was progress.

On another front, we were able to get the provincial development committee, the provincial coordination centre, district development assemblies, policy advisory groups and community development councils up and running, admittedly with varying degrees of success. We instituted an RC South Regional Governance Conference of agencies, which by the time we left met regularly on their own to share challenges and best practices. Not exciting stuff, but central to the foundation of a civil society, especially one as complex as this. During Operation Medusa, these institutions gave the people proof that their leaders were working on their behalf and helped them appreciate that those claiming to represent them would indeed take action against a determined enemy. Even better, they would win. Before Medusa, people had lost confidence in their leaders. As a subsequent national opinion survey revealed, by the time it was over that confidence had been re-established. That was one of the enduring benefits of the operation.

We certainly did not comprehend the Taliban yearly cycle when we arrived. Our plans were written under the presumption that the peak fighting season would be at the beginning of the summer each year, whereas when we actually fought them, we learned that their peak fighting period was during September and October. We came to that conclusion only late in the tour, by which time we were already into Operation Medusa. The news reports stated at the time that the insurgence was getting stronger. We knew where the Taliban were and what we needed to do. Just as a cancer-killing medicine will make a patient feel worse at first, our routing of the Taliban in RC South disturbed the people, the terrain, the dwellings and the economy. The southern provinces in general and Panjwayi in particular were the sanctuary in which the Taliban had long operated without interference. So things looked worse once we began. And the more we put pressure on them, the harder they came after us. We were playing chicken; the question was who would swerve first?

Taliban leaders who came from Pakistan were the true enemies. Among those who sided with them, the average fighter was nothing more than an impoverished Afghan trying to find a way to support a family. In no way were these people our enemy. Differentiating between the two groups was often impossible and caused us great anguish. We did everything we could not to rack up a body count. In return, they did their utmost to destroy and attack us wherever we were. The Taliban did everything to prove their superiority and discredit whatever we did. They ran a dirty campaign of innuendo and accusation against the Afghan authorities and the international coalition, who they painted as self-interested invaders. We built and rebuilt bridges and district centres over and over again, in part just to underscore the point that we were not going to be deterred. And we were not. Throughout the tour, culminating with Operation Medusa, the Taliban were defeated in every tactical engagement.

Contrary to what you see at the movies, no military operation goes perfectly. Far from it. The Taliban were a formidable, real-life enemy who had a strategy and knew their tactics. They were intent on taking the region and then the country. They were also agile. As we saw in August and September 2006, they could change their tactics radically to exploit what they perceived to be a weakness on our part, so we had to evolve just as rapidly when actions on the ground indicated a shift in their approach. Once you engage with the enemy, the key is to be guided by a plan that takes you to the desired outcome—in our case to defeat the enemy in Panjwayi. None of us believed that it would go smoothly. By this time in our tour we fully grasped the need for detailed and dynamic planning and nimble execution. After some early setbacks, we drove hard and took every opportunity to move forward. Not one of us had the advantage of complete information, context or understanding of the overall situation, but we did achieve what desperately needed to be done, albeit at a very high cost.

> Medusa was a great success tactically and Canadians fought and died and succeeded, but like all battles, it had its moments. On occasions, it was a very close run and that's war. The fact is they won. That's what you've got to keep hanging on to. People came through and learned. Soldiers who on day one were scared shitless, by day eight were standing strong and effective in the middle of the Taliban position.
>
> DAVID RICHARDS

Criticism of individuals during any operation, especially Operation Medusa, is unfair. The sheer complexity of this operation, the competing demands from nations, the enemy and the Afghan leadership meant that this fight was never going to be straightforward. At the battalion and task-force level, this was a tactical slog on difficult terrain against significant enemy numbers. At the regional and ISAF levels, this was tactical, strategic and political as nations declared what they could and could not do. The limitations on the scope of our activity, along with the restricted time we had to use our borrowed resources, made this difficult mission even harder to prosecute. Operation Medusa put pressure on everyone, and the higher up you went, the more complex the problem on the ground became.

Given the enemy and the changing conditions, it was not surprising that disagreements were commonplace. These were never personal and were always about difficult situations that involved national requirements, cultural ways of doing things, difficult decisions made under time constraints or high-risk situations. This was combat, and when everything was added up the pressures on everyone from the commanders all the way down to the soldier in the front line cannot be overstressed. I have never before or since felt that much pressure or been under the level of scrutiny to deliver effects in the craziest situations imaginable. You couldn't make this stuff up. If in training we had received the scenarios we actually faced during our tour, we would have laughed.

But this was no laughing matter. In the middle of the fight during Operation Medusa, a British Nimrod aircraft crashed, killing all onboard. We dealt with death every day, managed political demands and time-constraint requirements, and sometimes, often, there were disagreements. Ben Freakley and I had many lively discussions. Omer and I had lively discussions. Ian and I had lively discussions. Every one of us no doubt had a lively discussion with everyone else in theatre at some stage or another. This was not Ottawa, Washington or London. This was combat, and people's lives were at stake every day. Without frank discussion the outcomes could have been disastrous. The pressure and mental fatigue affected us all—commanders, staff and, most of all, our superb soldiers on the front lines. We all wanted to win and we all disagreed daily on how that should be done. Thank God we did. I can say with confidence that the final outcome of every situation was based on a combination of the opinions expressed.

NATO was not immune to the pressures of the theatre or mission. The coalition was tested through national rules of engagement, national caveats, limited capabilities, limited operational experience, and limitations in intelligence-sharing outside of the so-called five-eyes community of Americans, Brits, Canadians, Australians and New Zealanders. Operation Medusa provided something more than what was found on the battlefield. It provided SACEUR General Jim Jones with the ammunition to talk to the NATO coalition partners about stated and unstated limitations. Or, in plain language, what you say versus what you are prepared to deliver when it comes to the crunch. Little in NATO changed as a result of Operation Medusa, but our operation put the coalition on notice that troops in the field need the latitude and support to do what is necessary to fight the realities on the ground, particularly when in close combat. As for the troops on the ground, they all did what they were asked to do and succeeded in defeating the enemy.

Why did we succeed? Simply because we worked together. Working together and understanding the requirements ensured that things got done. The Canadians provided critical support to the inflow of the British in Helmand and the Dutch and Romanian troops into RC South. Both the Dutch and British were able to arrive without incurring any casualties. The Americans ensured that Canada had the capabilities we needed until our critical equipment arrived in theatre. The Americans, British and Dutch sent badly needed forces to the Operation Medusa fight. Without those resources we would not have had the force ratios necessary to deal with the Taliban.

The Afghan National Army developed the most during our time there. Under General Raufi the 205th Corps improved incrementally on many fronts. When we arrived, they had shown little or no planning capability; yet, when we left they had evolved a planning discipline. When I later returned once to visit they were conducting routine rehearsal of concept (ROC) drills and, by my second visit, were conducting major operations on their own. They weren't perfect, but they were improving.

I am sorry to report that, in our time, the Afghan National Police were corrupt and, therefore, lacked credibility with the locals. No coalition soldier wanted to work with the ANP. They were unreliable and, more dangerously, an impediment to operations. The ANP was not a defined training priority when we arrived, and only in the later part of our tour did the Americans fund their development. As I had appreciated early on, policing should have been a priority. Thugs that they were, the Taliban posed both a community policing problem and a military threat. In such a scenario a competent police force working in partnership with a military coalition might have worked wonders.

The learning never stopped during the tour. Conflicts are evolutionary, and we had to evolve to meet the ever-changing enemy threat. We added new capabilities. We changed our equipment. We shifted our tactics. We picked up the pace of our thinking and acting to get ahead of the enemy and keep them off balance. Those who joined us without operational experience had to learn even more quickly than we had to. Whatever qualifications they brought with them meant nothing on their own; only front-line experience would make them smart, wary, tough and effective.

As one would expect, our experience subsequently informed the training of the Canadian military, training that became more demanding and more often conducted by those able to share their practical experience with the next crew destined to go into theatre. Training for operations always tends to focus on the last conflict, teaching the lessons learned from previous missions. But the operational tempo of training can seldom match that of combat.

> One of the reasons we ran our close-protection training in the United States was to escape the nearly crippling Canadian over-emphasis on what they considered safety which, while understandable, made running true reality-based training almost impossible.
>
> ADAM "SEEGY" SEEGMILLER

While the stark pressure of real operations can rarely be replicated, any organization that does not try to do so will soon be schooled in their

Adam "Seegy" Seegmiller was one of those who joined us (we called them "augmentees") following the tragic deaths of four of our comrades in April 2006. Seegy had an attitude that was simply
contagious, and he fit in with the Posse with ease. Seegy managed what most augmentees could
not—being wholly accepted by the family after a loss. He became one of our go-to lads, as he had
a good tactical sense about him and was someone that I quickly got to know and rely upon. It was
a joy to work with him.

folly by an enemy who knows that pressure better. The Canadian Armed Forces learned and improved after Medusa. They adapted faster than I had ever seen in the twenty-five years of my military career.

So was it worth it? Let's consider that. Operation Medusa was a costly and necessary fight that achieved a temporary effect that allowed the coalition and the Afghans to move on. We did not lose this battle. Had we, the consequences would have been grave. The Taliban would have proven the inability of the Afghan leadership to govern; NATO would have been seen as an entity incapable of either protecting or fighting; Canada would have borne the brunt of the criticism for NATO's failure; and certainly there would have been political fallout in Canada, the UK and the Netherlands, all of which were administered by minority governments at the time. Avoiding failure was more critical than winning, and we did not fail. The Afghan people saw their democratically elected leaders deploy a national army to protect the highest national goals during this battle. While conducted at great expense, Operation Medusa gave hope and opportunity to people, two precious gifts we all take for granted in Canada. The Canadian men and women who gave their lives did not die in vain, and those who were wounded may bear their scars with well-deserved pride. While the Taliban would come back more determined and in a form more sinister than before, using IEDs and suicide bombs with renewed determination, in Operation Medusa they had lost the hearts and minds of the Afghans.

At the time of writing, a legitimate, elected government of Afghanistan still continues to lead the country. The governments of Kandahar and all five other provinces in RC South are still securely in power. The nation's security forces still stand guard. It did not have to end that well, but it did. The battle was messy, complicated, convoluted, political, tactical, dynamic and frustrating. It was what it was. We all fought through this and, in my view, came out the other side as winners. Not winners at the end of a game but winners of one hand in the middle of a very long game.

WEEP

O ne aspect of the mission that none of us welcomed yet had to accept was that there were going to be casualties. The horrible truth of any conflict is that operations will put men and women at risk. There is no way that risk can be taken down to zero. It can be mitigated through many means but, inevitably, operations such as the one we undertook together in Afghanistan will result in losses.

In anticipation of this cold reality, we spent considerable time with our command teams and soldiers learning how to respond when deaths and injuries occur. We did as much as we could to get ready for those tragic events. We met with experts including Dave Grossman, author of *On Killing*. We refined procedures to manage these scenarios and rehearsed them repeatedly.

As part of our preparations, we considered how we would approach breaking sad news, both in theatre and to families at home. I directed that bad news would be given by me, an unpleasant duty but nothing compared to the anguish suffered by a loved one. During our tour, whenever soldiers perished I wrote and sent letters of condolence to their families. At our base on Kandahar Airfield we gathered for solemn services to honour fallen comrades as the flags of their nations flew above us. And as we readied each soldier for his or her final flight home to Canada, we made our farewells at ramp ceremonies, each time a sober reminder of the seriousness of our mission and the importance of doing everything in our power to mitigate risk.

Ramp ceremonies were emotional events that happened far too often. Whenever a soldier was killed, we held a ramp ceremony at Kandahar Airfield, attended by all available soldiers. The purpose was to pay our respects to a fallen comrade. Every nation's men and women would attend, without exception. These were big events involving hundreds—if not a thousand—soldiers, and they constantly got bigger throughout our tour. The security aspect was always a concern, and we mitigated the potential for a rocket attack by varying the time they took place. Each ramp ceremony was conducted in a similar fashion. An aircraft would be positioned to receive the remains, and soldiers from every contingent would line up on either side right up to the aircraft. Comrades from the unit which had lost the soldier or soldiers would position themselves to the right of the aircraft, with the senior commanders of RC South across from them. The coffins would be paraded up between the ranks, carried by fellow soldiers. The padre would be at the front and say a few prayers before the remains were taken on board the aircraft. A few minutes were set aside for fellow soldiers to go onto the aircraft to say their farewells. "Amazing Grace" was played at every ceremony that I recall. Today, when I hear "Amazing Grace," I remember those ramp ceremonies. I recall that I attended a ramp ceremony the week I arrived in Afghanistan, and I attended a ramp ceremony the week I left. There is not a day that goes by that I do not think of all the soldiers who were killed during our tour. I wrote to every family of our fallen heroes. We sent a flag from the nation of the soldier to the family as a tribute to the hero. These ceremonies were conducted with the utmost respect, and there was a pouring out of emotions and support from every nation. Every soldier touched the lives of everyone.

Randy Payne and Matt Dinning hung around together and they were part of the family. Both were good-humoured and were consummate professionals. They quietly went about their jobs and allowed me to do mine. I was never concerned about my safety with these fine police officers around me. Their loss was gut-wrenching and there is not a day that I do not think about them. We celebrated the tenth anniversary of their death at the Military Police School in Borden. For the first time since Afghanistan, most of the Posse gathered. I spoke in front of the Police Academy staff and students, and highlighted the leadership and professionalism that these two fine soldiers exhibited. They were the best that the academy produced and exemplified what it means to be Military Police.

Having written to the family of every service member killed, as the tour was ending I felt a growing responsibility to visit, or at least offer to visit, each family in turn once we arrived back in Canada. Our brigade sergeant major Mike MacDonald, my executive assistant David Buchanan and I agreed we had an obligation to pay our personal respects to each family and answer any questions they had regarding their loved one. During those visits we would be able to ask if everything that could be done was being done for them.

About half the families accepted our request to visit. After the tour the three of us set out as a team. With details of each incident in hand we offered to answer candidly any questions they might have. These were all difficult visits, yet we were amazed by the common courage and resilience of the families of the fallen. Never have we been so proud as we were to be in the presence of those people we met across Canada, including the families of the four comrades we lost from the Posse. We also heard stories of the magnificent performance of the home units that supported families of deployed soldiers in time of great distress.

On those visits we learned that some widows were in danger of losing their homes. While they had paid for mortgage insurance assuming it would cover them for that unthinkable day, they were about to lose everything because of a war-exclusion clause inserted into the fine print of their policies. We were aghast.

On one of our stops in Toronto, I asked to see anyone in the banking or insurance industry who was ready to listen to a sad story. At the Royal Canadian Military Institute we met with half a dozen business leaders, including Blake Goldring, chairman and CEO of the investment management firm AGF. These executives too were aghast. We suggested that this unfair exclusion was not the deliberate act of any underwriter, but likely just the blanket application of an overly general provision. They asked us for the names of the affected families. In the following days we double-checked and identified even more families adversely affected by this regulation. Blake and his colleagues took it upon themselves to do the right thing. The families affected did not lose their homes and, a couple of years later, the unfair war-exclusion clause was changed; it no longer applies to personnel of either the Canadian Armed Forces or the RCMP. As such, our visits were a series of sad events that generated a few happy results.

Paying respects to the families of the fallen is one of the hardest things a commander must do. Words never come easily, for what can one really say to a family who has lost someone to the violence of war? A mere visit will never lessen the pain, but we did learn that just knowing more about what their loved one did and what difference they had made can give a measure of satisfaction that helps in some small way.

The years have ticked by since those visits, and there continue to be occasions on which my colleagues and I are able to visit again with the family members of our fallen comrades. I cherish those moments, for when we do meet, we have one more opportunity to celebrate the contributions of those who made the ultimate sacrifice.

To all of them, we dedicate this story.

This is a shot of the members of the Posse who went to Mizan, a district dominated by the Taliban in the northwest corner of Zabul Province. Into that heart of insurgent influence we injected an American platoon of some sixty soldiers, augmented by a Romanian mortar section. In my daily operational updates, I heard how disruptive this group of soldiers were being to the Taliban, and what positive progress they were making with the local Afghan authorities. They had taken to their task with fervour. We decided to fly up for a couple of days to see for ourselves what effects they were producing. Commanded by a young American lieutenant, the platoon in Mizan was executing an impressive, balanced reinforcement of the Governor of Zabul's intent. Their effect was so strong that, in retaliation, the Taliban were attacking their outpost every night. When we first arrived in Mizan we met with the mayor. With him was the chief of police, a colourful character known by all as Crazybones, who lived on the wild side, with a meaty SPG-9 Russian recoilless anti-tank rifle as his personal sidearm. The day was productive. Our patrol into town went without incident, but for the fatal shooting of one person over some tribal disagreement. That night we were awoken by a barrage of incoming small-arms and machine-gun fire, as well as RPGs and other munitions. Everyone scrambled to their assigned positions for one of the most intensive firefights we had throughout the tour. The American lieutenant calmly handled the situation, including reporting back to headquarters and the coordination of fast air, which was then dispatched to the scene. The Romanians fully engaged with their 82mm mortar, as did the Americans. Quite the night. Here, photographed in the calm of the next morning, are (left to right) Tucker, Boss, Dooner, Project Bryant, Seegy and Bomber (who took the photo). Just another typical day in RC South.

HONOUR OUR FALLEN

More than 40,000 Canadian soldiers, sailors, aviators and special forces operators served in Afghanistan from 2001 until late 2014. They came from all walks of life and from every corner of our country. They trained hard and worked furiously, gallantly exercising their talent and insight for the benefit of the people of Afghanistan. All risked their health and their lives. Some 2,000 soldiers were wounded or injured, and 159 Canadian Armed Forces personnel and 162 Canadians in total gave their lives in service to their country and the world. Here we remember our fallen. May these noble Canadians rest in peace, and may their names forever be commemorated by those who cherish courage, duty and honour.

April 18, 2002	**Private Nathan Smith**
	3rd Battalion, Princess Patricia's Canadian Light Infantry
April 18, 2002	**Private Richard Green**
	3rd Battalion, Princess Patricia's Canadian Light Infantry
April 18, 2002	**Corporal Ainsworth Dyer**
	3rd Battalion, Princess Patricia's Canadian Light Infantry
April 18, 2002	**Sergeant Marc D. Léger**
	3rd Battalion, Princess Patricia's Canadian Light Infantry
October 2, 2003	**Sergeant Robert Alan Short**
	3rd Battalion, The Royal Canadian Regiment

October 2, 2003 **Corporal Robbie Christopher Beerenfenger**
3rd Battalion, The Royal Canadian Regiment

January 27, 2004 **Corporal Jamie Brendan Murphy**
1st Battalion, The Royal Canadian Regiment

August 27, 2005 **Corporal Jacques Joseph Andre Larocque**
8 Wing Air Maintenance Squadron

November 24, 2005 **Private Braun Scott Woodfield**
2nd Battalion, The Royal Canadian Regiment

January 15, 2006 **Mr. Glyn Berry**
Foreign Affairs Canada

March 2, 2006 **Corporal Paul Davis**
2nd Battalion, Princess Patricia's Canadian Light Infantry

March 4, 2006 **Master Corporal Timothy Wilson**
2nd Battalion, Princess Patricia's Canadian Light Infantry

March 29, 2006 **Private Robert Costall**
1st Battalion, Princess Patricia's Canadian Light Infantry

April 22, 2006 **Lieutenant William Turner**
20th Field Artillery Regiment

April 22, 2006 **Corporal Randy Payne**
1 Garrison Military Police Company

April 22, 2006 **Bombardier Myles Stanley John Mansell**
5th British Columbia Field Artillery Regiment

April 22, 2006 **Corporal Matthew David James Dinning**
2 Military Police Platoon

May 17, 2006 **Captain Nichola Kathleen Sarah Goddard**
1st Royal Canadian Horse Artillery

July 9, 2006 **Corporal Anthony Joseph Boneca**
The Lake Superior Scottish Regiment

July 22, 2006 **Corporal Jason Patrick Warren**
The Black Watch (Royal Highland Regiment) of Canada

July 22, 2006 **Corporal Francisco Gomez**
1st Battalion, Princess Patricia's Canadian Light Infantry

August 3, 2006 **Corporal Christopher Jonathan Reid**
1st Battalion, Princess Patricia's Canadian Light Infantry

August 3, 2006	**Corporal Bryce Jeffrey Keller**
	1st Battalion, Princess Patricia's Canadian Light Infantry
August 3, 2006	**Sergeant Vaughan Ingram**
	1st Battalion, Princess Patricia's Canadian Light Infantry
August 3, 2006	**Private Kevin Dallaire**
	1st Battalion, Princess Patricia's Canadian Light Infantry
August 5, 2006	**Master Corporal Raymond Arndt**
	The Loyal Edmonton Regiment
August 9, 2006	**Master Corporal Jeffrey Scott Walsh**
	2nd Battalion, Princess Patricia's Canadian Light Infantry
August 11, 2006	**Corporal Andrew James Eykelenboom**
	1st Field Ambulance
August 22, 2006	**Corporal David Braun**
	2nd Battalion, Princess Patricia's Canadian Light Infantry
September 3, 2006	**Sergeant Shane Stachnik**
	2 Combat Engineer Regiment
September 3, 2006	**Warrant Officer Richard Francis Nolan**
	1st Battalion, The Royal Canadian Regiment
September 3, 2006	**Warrant Officer Frank Robert Mellish**
	1st Battalion, The Royal Canadian Regiment
September 3, 2006	**Private William Jonathan James Cushley**
	1st Battalion, The Royal Canadian Regiment
September 4, 2006	**Private Mark Anthony Graham**
	1st Battalion, The Royal Canadian Regiment
September 18, 2006	**Corporal Keith Morley**
	2nd Battalion, Princess Patricia's Canadian Light Infantry
September 18, 2006	**Corporal Shane Keating**
	2nd Battalion, Princess Patricia's Canadian Light Infantry
September 18, 2006	**Private David Byers**
	2nd Battalion, Princess Patricia's Canadian Light Infantry
September 18, 2006	**Corporal Glen Arnold**
	2 Field Ambulance
September 29, 2006	**Private Josh Klukie**
	1st Battalion, The Royal Canadian Regiment

October 3, 2006	**Corporal Robert Thomas James Mitchell**
	The Royal Canadian Dragoons
October 3, 2006	**Sergeant Craig Paul Gillam**
	The Royal Canadian Dragoons
October 7, 2006	**Trooper Mark Andrew Wilson**
	The Royal Canadian Dragoons
October 14, 2006	**Private Blake Neil Williamson**
	1st Battalion, The Royal Canadian Regiment
October 14, 2006	**Sergeant Darcy Scott Tedford**
	1st Battalion, The Royal Canadian Regiment
November 27, 2006	**Corporal Albert Storm**
	1st Battalion, The Royal Canadian Regiment
November 27, 2006	**Chief Warrant Officer Robert Girouard**
	1st Battalion, The Royal Canadian Regiment
March 6, 2007	**Corporal Kevin Megeney**
	1st Battalion, The Nova Scotia Highlanders
April 8, 2007	**Private Kevin Vincent Kennedy**
	2nd Battalion, The Royal Canadian Regiment
April 8, 2007	**Private David Robert Greenslade**
	2nd Battalion, The Royal Canadian Regiment
April 8, 2007	**Corporal Aaron Edward Williams**
	2nd Battalion, The Royal Canadian Regiment
April 8, 2007	**Corporal Christopher Paul Stannix**
	The Princess Louise Fusiliers
April 8, 2007	**Corporal Brent Donald Poland**
	2nd Battalion, The Royal Canadian Regiment
April 8, 2007	**Sergeant Donald Lucas**
	2nd Battalion, The Royal Canadian Regiment
April 11, 2007	**Trooper Patrick James Pentland**
	The Royal Canadian Dragoons
April 11, 2007	**Master Corporal Allan Stewart**
	The Royal Canadian Dragoons
April 18, 2007	**Master Corporal Anthony Klumpenhouwer**
	Canadian Special Operations Forces Command

May 25, 2007	Corporal Matthew McCully
	2 Canadian Mechanized Brigade Group Headquarters and Signals Squadron
May 30, 2007	Master Corporal Darrell Jason Priede
	Army News Team, 3 Area Support Group
June 11, 2007	Trooper Darryl Caswell
	The Royal Canadian Dragoons
June 20, 2007	Private Joel Vincent Wiebe
	3rd Battalion, Princess Patricia's Canadian Light Infantry
June 20, 2007	Corporal Stephen Frederick Bouzane
	3rd Battalion, Princess Patricia's Canadian Light Infantry
June 20, 2007	Sergeant Christos Karigiannis
	3rd Battalion, Princess Patricia's Canadian Light Infantry
July 4, 2007	Private Lane William Thomas Watkins
	3rd Battalion, Princess Patricia's Canadian Light Infantry
July 4, 2007	Corporal Cole D. Bartsch
	3rd Battalion, Princess Patricia's Canadian Light Infantry
July 4, 2007	Master Corporal Colin Stuart Francis Bason
	The Royal Westminster Regiment
July 4, 2007	Captain Matthew Johnathan Dawe
	3rd Battalion, Princess Patricia's Canadian Light Infantry
July 4, 2007	Corporal Jordan Anderson
	3rd Battalion, Princess Patricia's Canadian Light Infantry
July 4, 2007	Captain Jefferson Clifford Francis
	1 Royal Canadian Horse Artillery
August 19, 2007	Private Simon Longtin
	3rd Battalion, Royal 22nd Regiment
August 22, 2007	Master Warrant Officer Mario Mercier
	3rd Battalion, Royal 22nd Regiment
August 22, 2007	Master Warrant Officer Christian Duchesne
	5 Field Ambulance
August 29, 2007	Major Raymond Mark Ruckpaul
	The Royal Canadian Dragoons
September 24, 2007	Corporal Nathan Hornburg
	The King's Own Calgary Regiment

November 17, 2007	**Corporal Nicolas Raymond Beauchamp**
	5 Field Ambulance
November 17, 2007	**Private Michel Jr. Lévesque**
	3rd Battalion, Royal 22nd Regiment
December 30, 2007	**Gunner Jonathan Dion**
	5th Régiment d'artillerie légère du Canada
January 6, 2008	**Corporal Éric Labbé**
	2nd Battalion, Royal 22nd Regiment
January 6, 2008	**Warrant Officer Hani Massouh**
	2nd Battalion, Royal 22nd Regiment
January 15, 2008	**Trooper Richard Renaud**
	12e Régiment blindé du Canada
January 23, 2008	**Sapper Etienne Gonthier**
	5 Combat Engineer Regiment
March 2, 2008	**Trooper Michael Yuki Hayakaze**
	Lord Strathcona's Horse (Royal Canadians)
March 11, 2008	**Bombardier Jérémie Ouellet**
	1st Regiment, Royal Canadian Horse Artillery
March 16, 2008	**Sergeant Jason Boyes**
	2nd Battalion, Princess Patricia's Canadian Light Infantry
April 4, 2008	**Private Terry John Street**
	2nd Battalion, Princess Patricia's Canadian Light Infantry
May 6, 2008	**Corporal Michael Starker**
	15 Edmonton Field Ambulance Regiment
June 3, 2008	**Captain Richard Steven Leary**
	2nd Battalion, Princess Patricia's Canadian Light Infantry
June 7, 2008	**Captain Jonathan Sutherland Snyder**
	1st Battalion, Princess Patricia's Canadian Light Infantry
July 4, 2008	**Corporal Brendan Anthony Downey**
	15 Wing Military Police Detachment
July 5, 2008	**Private Colin William Wilmot**
	1 Field Ambulance
July 18, 2008	**Corporal James Hayward Arnal**
	2nd Battalion, Princess Patricia's Canadian Light Infantry

August 9, 2008	Master Corporal Joshua Brian Roberts
	2nd Battalion, Princess Patricia's Canadian Light Infantry
August 11, 2008	Master Corporal Erin Doyle
	3rd Battalion, Princess Patricia's Canadian Light Infantry
August 20, 2008	Sergeant Shawn Allen Eades
	1 Combat Engineer Regiment
August 20, 2008	Corporal Dustin Roy Robert Joseph Wasden
	1 Combat Engineer Regiment
August 20, 2008	Sapper Stephan John Stock
	1 Combat Engineer Regiment
September 3, 2008	Private Chadwick James Horn
	2nd Battalion, Princess Patricia's Canadian Light Infantry
September 3, 2008	Corporal Michael James Alexander Seggie
	2nd Battalion, Princess Patricia's Canadian Light Infantry
September 3, 2008	Corporal Andrew Paul Grenon
	2nd Battalion, Princess Patricia's Canadian Light Infantry
September 7, 2008	Sergeant Prescott Shipway
	2nd Battalion, Princess Patricia's Canadian Light Infantry
December 5, 2008	Private Demetrios Diplaros
	1st Battalion, The Royal Canadian Regiment
December 5, 2008	Corporal Mark Robert McLaren
	1st Battalion, The Royal Canadian Regiment
December 5, 2008	Warrant Officer Robert John Wilson
	1st Battalion, The Royal Canadian Regiment
December 13, 2008	Private John Michael Roy Curwin
	2nd Battalion, The Royal Canadian Regiment
December 13, 2008	Private Justin Peter Jones
	2nd Battalion, The Royal Canadian Regiment
December 13, 2008	Corporal Thomas James Hamilton
	2nd Battalion, The Royal Canadian Regiment
December 26, 2008	Private Michael Bruce Freeman
	3rd Battalion, The Royal Canadian Regiment
December 27, 2008	Warrant Officer Gaétan Joseph Roberge
	2nd Battalion, Royal 22nd Regiment

December 27, 2008	**Sergeant Gregory John Kruse**
	2 Combat Engineer Regiment
January 7, 2009	**Trooper Brian Richard Good**
	3rd Battalion, The Royal Canadian Regiment
January 31, 2009	**Sapper Sean David Greenfield**
	2 Combat Engineer Regiment
March 3, 2009	**Corporal Kenneth Chad O'Quinn**
	2 Canadian Mechanized Brigade Group Headquarters and Signals Squadron
March 3, 2009	**Corporal Dany Olivier Fortin**
	425 Tactical Fighter Squadron
March 3, 2009	**Warrant Officer Dennis Raymond Brown**
	The Lincoln and Welland Regiment
March 8, 2009	**Trooper Marc Diab**
	The Royal Canadian Dragoons
March 20, 2009	**Trooper Corey Joseph Hayes**
	The Royal Canadian Dragoons
March 20, 2009	**Trooper Jack Bouthillier**
	The Royal Canadian Dragoons
March 20, 2009	**Corporal Tyler Crooks**
	3rd Battalion, The Royal Canadian Regiment
March 20, 2009	**Master Corporal Scott Francis Vernelli**
	3rd Battalion, The Royal Canadian Regiment
April 13, 2009	**Trooper Karine Blais**
	12th Régiment blindé du Canada
April 23, 2009	**Major Michelle Mendes**
	Defence Intelligence
June 8, 2009	**Private Alexandre Péloquin**
	3rd Battalion, Royal 22nd Regiment
June 14, 2009	**Corporal Martin Dubé**
	5 Combat Engineer Regiment
July 3, 2009	**Corporal Nicholas Bulger**
	3rd Battalion, Princess Patricia's Canadian Light Infantry
July 4, 2009	**Master Corporal Charles-Philippe Michaud**
	2nd Battalion, Royal 22nd Regiment

July 6, 2009	**Corporal Martin Joannette**
	3rd Battalion, Royal 22nd Regiment
July 6, 2009	**Master Corporal Patrice Audet**
	430 Tactical Helicopter Squadron
July 16, 2009	**Private Sébastien Courcy**
	2nd Battalion, Royal 22nd Regiment
August 1, 2009	**Corporal Christian Bobbitt**
	5 Combat Engineer Regiment
August 1, 2009	**Sapper Matthieu Allard**
	5 Combat Engineer Regiment
September 6, 2009	**Major Yannick Pépin**
	5 Combat Engineer Regiment
September 6, 2009	**Corporal Jean-François Drouin**
	5 Combat Engineer Regiment
September 13, 2009	**Private Patrick Lormand**
	2nd Battalion, Royal 22nd Regiment
September 17, 2009	**Private Jonathan Couturier**
	2nd Battalion, Royal 22nd Regiment
October 28, 2009	**Lieutenant Justin Boyes**
	3rd Battalion, Princess Patricia's Canadian Light Infantry
October 30, 2009	**Sapper Steven Marshall**
	1 Combat Engineer Regiment
December 23, 2009	**Lieutenant Andrew Nuttall**
	1st Battalion, Princess Patricia's Canadian Light Infantry
December 30, 2009	**Sergeant George Miok**
	41 Combat Engineer Regiment
December 30, 2009	**Sergeant Kirk Taylor**
	84 Independent Field Battery, Royal Canadian Artillery
December 30, 2009	**Corporal Zachery McCormack**
	The Loyal Edmonton Regiment
December 30, 2009	**Private Garrett William Chidley**
	2nd Battalion, Princess Patricia's Canadian Light Infantry
January 16, 2010	**Sergeant John Faught**
	1st Battalion, Princess Patricia's Canadian Light Infantry

February 10, 2010	**Captain Frank Paul**
	28 Field Ambulance
February 12, 2010	**Corporal Joshua Caleb Baker**
	The Loyal Edmonton Regiment
March 20, 2010	**Corporal Darren James Fitzpatrick**
	3rd Battalion, Princess Patricia's Canadian Light Infantry
April 11, 2010	**Private Tyler William Todd**
	1st Battalion, Princess Patricia's Canadian Light Infantry
May 3, 2010	**Petty Officer Craig Blake**
	Fleet Diving Unit (Atlantic)
May 14, 2010	**Private Kevin Thomas McKay**
	1st Battalion, Princess Patricia's Canadian Light Infantry
May 18, 2010	**Colonel Geoff Parker**
	Land Force Central Area Headquarters
May 24, 2010	**Trooper Larry Rudd**
	The Royal Canadian Dragoons
June 6, 2010	**Sergeant Martin Goudreault**
	1 Combat Engineer Regiment
June 21, 2010	**Sergeant James Patrick MacNeil**
	2 Combat Engineer Regiment
June 26, 2010	**Private Andrew Miller**
	2 Field Ambulance
June 26, 2010	**Master Corporal Kristal Giesebrecht**
	1 Canadian Field Hospital
July 20, 2010	**Sapper Brian Collier**
	1 Combat Engineer Regiment
August 30, 2010	**Corporal Brian Pinksen**
	2nd Battalion, Royal Newfoundland Regiment
December 18, 2010	**Corporal Steve Martin**
	3rd Battalion, Royal 22nd Regiment
March 27, 2011	**Corporal Yannick Scherrer**
	1st Battalion, Royal 22nd Regiment
May 27, 2011	**Bombardier Karl Manning**
	5th Régiment d'artillerie légère du Canada

June 25, 2011   **Master Corporal Francis Roy**

Canadian Special Operations Regiment

October 29, 2011   **Master Corporal Byron Garth Greff**

3rd Battalion, Princess Patricia's Canadian Light Infantry

January 17, 2014   **Mr. Martin Glazer**

Samson & Associates

January 17, 2014   **Mr. Peter McSheffrey**

Samson & Associates

TRACK OUR FRIENDS

WHERE ARE THEY NOW?

DAVID RICHARDS went on to command the British Army and then serve as Chief of the Defence Staff for the United Kingdom. For outstanding service to his country, David was elevated as Baron Richards of Herstmonceux. Lord Richards now resides in the pleasant seaside town of Emsworth in southern England, where he and his wife Caroline enjoy their family, sailing, and private-sector work. Whenever we visit England, my wife and I make a point of dropping in on my dear friend and former commander.

OMER LAVOIE went on to command the Counter-IED Task Force after Afghanistan. He commanded the 4th Canadian Division (Ontario) and is now a major general and commander of the 1st Canadian Division Headquarters located in Kingston, Ontario.

IAN HOPE went to CENTCOM as our Canadian liaison officer, and then attended the United States Army War College and worked with AFRICOM. Ian is now a colonel teaching at the NATO Defense College in Rome where he shares his experience and insight with the next generation of leaders.

MIKE WRIGHT went on to command the 2nd Battalion PPCLI and is now a colonel commanding 2 Canadian Mechanized Brigade Group in

Petawawa, Ontario. Mike has not lost his sense of humour and continues to be a great example of leadership to thousands of troops today.

BILL "MOTHER" IRVING returned (with his Harley mirrors) shortly after Operation Medusa to take his warrant officer's course in Gagetown, New Brunswick. He rejoined his regiment, eventually retiring from the regular force in 2014. Bill and his family then moved to Kingston where he continued to serve in the Army Reserve. Today he is regimental sergeant major for the Ontario Regiment in Oshawa. Having heard plenty of complaints in his time, he also acts as a complaint-management services agent for the Department of National Defence. Once a soldier, always a soldier, Mother continues to take care of his troops.

KARL EIKENBERRY served as Deputy Chairman of the NATO Military Committee. He became the U.S. Ambassador to Afghanistan from April 2009 to July 2011. I had the chance to visit him both at NATO and back in Afghanistan. He is now the Oksenberg-Rohlen Fellow and Director of the U.S. Asia Security Initiative at the Walter H. Shorenstein Asia-Pacific Research Center, and is a member of other prestigious faculties as well.

BEN FREAKLEY went on following Afghanistan to be the commanding general of Accessions Command until he retired in 2012. Ben went back to teaching others. He is now the special advisor to the president of Arizona State University, and is responsible for Leadership Initiatives at the McCain Institute for International Leadership in Washington, D.C.

RICK HILLIER retired in 2008 as Canada's Chief of the Defence Staff. He served as the chancellor of his alma mater, Memorial University of Newfoundland, and wrote two bestselling books on leadership and his time as the CDS. Rick speaks publicly on leadership, supports soldiers to this day, sits on the advisory board for Provincial Aerospace, and still tells the most compelling stories. I doubt he will ever slow down.

MIKE GAUTHIER continued to command CEFCOM until he retired in 2009, and is now a senior mentor at the Canadian Forces College in Toronto, passing along the wealth of knowledge and experience he acquired over years of senior command.

DON BOLDUC continued his stellar career and was soon promoted to brigadier general. He recently retired from the special forces community, and I am sure many bad guys out there are much relieved. Don is a now a leading advocate within the U.S. army for openness and innovation in the treatment of PTSD.

SHANE SCHREIBER went on to command the 2nd Battalion PPCLI, which I had the pleasure to see in action during the Olympics in Vancouver in 2010. He continues to be one of the most charismatic leaders I know. He is the author of *Shock Army of the British Empire: The Canadian Corps in the Last 100 Days of the Great War,* a wonderful read for any student of history. He is now the managing director of the Alberta Emergency Management Agency at the Government of Alberta in Edmonton.

DAVID "BUCK" BUCHANAN went on to a successful career in the CAF, including a posting as the Canadian liaison officer to the British Army. He retired in January 2017 and joined Canada's public service as a research officer in Kingston. He transferred to the Army Reserve and is now commanding officer of 30th Field Regiment, Royal Canadian Artillery in Ottawa.

DEREK PROHAR joined the Canadian Army Command and Staff College and is now commanding officer of 3 PPCLI. In his office he proudly displays the bulletproof, armoured plate that saved his life at Sperwan Ghar.

HARJIT SAJJAN returned to Afghanistan for two subsequent tours. He worked for my dear friend James Terry, who was deputy commander of 10th Mountain Division during our tour and who took Harj with him when he returned as the commander of 10th Mountain and RC South. Harj did his last tour in Kandahar Province with Jon Vance, Canada's current CDS. Harj went on to command his own home unit, the British Columbia Regiment. He entered federal politics in 2015, winning his seat in southern B.C., and then was named as Canada's Minister of National Defence.

ASADULLAH KHALID continued to serve as Governor of Kandahar until 2008. He then went on to serve as the Minister of Tribal and Border Affairs. In 2012 he was appointed as head of the National Directorate of Security (NDS), the Afghan secret service that had informed us about Taliban fatigue during Operation Medusa. There were several attempts on his life, the last of which severely injured him, forcing his retirement from the NDS in 2015.

MATTHEW SPRAGUE received the Meritorious Service Medal (Military Division), which is awarded to individuals whose specific achievements have brought honour to the Canadian Forces and to Canada. He became a lieutenant colonel and works with the army in Kingston.

GEOFF ABTHORPE went on to study at the Pakistan Command and Staff College, and then joined the Canadian Manoeuvre Centre in Wainwright as the chief plans officer. He left the regular force in 2014, moved to Thunder Bay, Ontario, and transferred to the Army Reserve. He now commands the 38 Canadian Brigade Group.

ADAM "SEEGY" SEEGMILLER still serves with the close protection unit within the Canadian Armed Forces. Highly regarded for his long practical experience, Adam has made great efforts to ensure that the training of mission-bound protection teams is based on a true understanding of the current threat.

ALLAN "DOONER" MULDOON is a reserve corporal living in Ottawa. Dooner has also become a City of Ottawa firefighter. He has not changed a bit. We always have a good laugh. Whenever we get together we reminisce about our various visits *outside the wire* when he was my personal body-guard in RC South.

STEVE WILLIAMS went back to Alaska, where he finished off his command tour with the National Guard. Two years after leading Task Force Grizzly into action in Operation Medusa, Steve was presented with Canada's Meritorious Service Medal (Military Division) for his hard work, bravery and professionalism. He retired from the army in 2009 and now resides in Colorado Springs. He is a broker and doing well.

MARK GASPAROTTO was awarded the Meritorious Service Medal for his leadership of 23 Field Squadron in Afghanistan. After the tour, he co-wrote *Clearing the Way: Combat Engineers in Kandahar*, which I recommend. After commanding 2 Combat Engineer Regiment, Mark was promoted to colonel and deployed to Haiti in 2016 as the task force commander during Operation Hamlet. Mark lives in Ottawa.

ANDY LUSSIER received the Meritorious Service Medal for his outstanding service rendered with his ISTAR squadron in RC South. He became chief instructor at the Armour School (RCACS), then chief of operations at the Combat Training Centre in Gagetown. He is currently commanding officer of personnel support services for the 5th Canadian Division Support Group.

MIKE "BOMBER" MACDONALD received the Meritorious Service Decoration for his steadfast leadership and went on to a successful career including teaching at the leadership academy in Europe. Mike retired and resides in Ottawa, from where he and his wife travel the world. He continues to play hockey to the chagrin of those who play against him. He remains the fit soldier that I always remember.

SIMON HETHERINGTON continues to serve in the CAF, where his career is still on the rise. He served in the United States as deputy commander for the

18th Airborne Corps and as the commander of the 3rd Canadian Division. I had the pleasure of seeing him in Edmonton before he moved to Kingston, whereupon after promotion to major general he now commands our Army and Doctrine Command. As always, our visits are filled with laughter and fine stories.

FRED LEWIS continued to enjoy great success, including postings as the commandant of the Canadian Army Command and Staff College, commander of Joint Task Force Jerusalem, and finally as commander of the 4th Canadian Division in Toronto. Fred retired in 2012 and moved with his family to just north of Kingston. Fred enjoys hunting, and we get together about once a year for a bird shoot. It is always good to see my former deputy.

DAVE HOUTHUYZEN is a sergeant posted to the Military Police Academy in Borden. Dave organized the tenth anniversary of our tour, and most of the Posse was able to attend the very moving ceremony at the MP Academy with other members of the MP community and their commanding officer, Lieutenant Colonel Adam Battista. I have visited the academy several times, and always take time to see Dave and his family.

TREVOR FRIESEN is now a major posted to 41 Combat Engineer Regiment in Edmonton.

GREG "MOONER" MOON is a warrant officer posted to the Combat Training Centre in Gagetown, New Brunswick. He works at the Armoured Corps School.

JEFF "JEB" HAWES is a sergeant posted to the Joint Personnel Support Unit in Halifax and is transitioning into retirement.

KEITH "BROWNIE" BROWN is a warrant officer posted to the 2nd Battalion, Royal Canadian Regiment in Gagetown, New Brunswick.

SHAWN WALSH is retired and residing in the Halifax area.

RICK TUCKER is a petty officer 2nd class posted to the west coast and is currently deployed.

KANE "PROJECT BRYANT" BRYANT is posted to 2 Military Police Regiment.

JAMIE OFFREY is a warrant officer posted to the Canadian Embassy in Belgrade.

MIKE "WOODY" WOODROW is retired and resides in New Brunswick.

JOHN "HODGY" HODGES is retired and resides in Ontario.

ARON POPE is retired and resides in Ontario.

READ OTHER BOOKS

A. BOOKS ABOUT AFGHANISTAN WORTH SAMPLING

The Bear Went Over the Mountain: Soviet Combat Tactics in Afghanistan
BY LIEUTENANT COLONEL LESTER W. GRAU

This is a book about the Soviet experiences in Afghanistan in which, along with its companion *The Other Side of the Mountain*, Les Grau captures what the Soviets and Afghans did in fighting each other. History teaches us the good and the bad, from which we can learn. Les Grau came to us before the mission to brief our command team on the concepts advanced in the books he had written. Learning from history allowed us to be better informed and aware of the complex culture we were about to enter. His books were key for me in understanding the Taliban intent and the age-old tradition in which Afghans fight people like us.

No Lack of Courage: Operation Medusa, Afghanistan
BY BERND HORN

Bernd was the first author who took the time to capture the key leaders' stories about what happened in Afghanistan. A military historian as well as an officer in the CAF, Bernd captured what we were thinking and what we did: the good, the bad, and the ugly. His work puts the pieces together so readers can understand the complexity of the Afghan fight.

The Unexpected War: Canada in Kandahar
BY JANICE GROSS STEIN AND EUGENE LANG
Janice and Eugene explore the overarching political framework that sent us to Afghanistan. They tell the story of what happened in the political arena in Ottawa, what the arguments were, and who played the key roles that shaped the decision for the mission. Their work demonstrates the vast difference between what Ottawa thought should happen and the realities of the conflict on the ground.

Fifteen Days: Stories of Bravery, Friendship, Life and Death from Inside the New Canadian Army
BY CHRISTIE BLATCHFORD
Christie was embedded with the first rotation in the south. Her observations show the struggles and tremendous courage of the men and women who fought every day. Politicians sent soldiers to war, and young Canadians threw their hearts into doing what Canadians believed in—bringing hope and opportunity to Afghans. Christie spent many weeks with the rank and file and, in her book, provides a tactical view of what the conflict was like from a soldier's perspective.

Outside the Wire: The War in Afghanistan in the Words of Its Participants
BY KEVIN PATTERSON AND JANE WARREN
An insightful account of the Afghan conflict from the soldiers' perspective.

Contact Charlie: The Canadian Army, the Taliban and the Battle that Saved Afghanistan
BY CHRIS WATTIE
Chris was there as a reporter, and his book about Charlie Company tells the story of the men and women who fought daily to bring peace and security to the region. Chris's understanding of the situation enables the

reader to feel the danger and challenges our Canadian soldiers felt every day that they were in Afghanistan.

Lions of Kandahar: The Story of a Fight Against All Odds
BY RUSTY BRADLEY AND KEVIN MAURER
This is a brilliant description of the battle in Panjwayi from an American view. The American special forces played a critical role alongside their Canadian brothers in arms. Together, the Canadians and Americans did the heavy lifting during Medusa. This is another great telling of that story.

Kandahar Tour: The Turning Point in Canada's Afghan Mission
BY LEE WINDSOR, DAVID CHARTERS AND BRENT WILSON
A well-written account of the role played by Task Force 3–06 in Kandahar Province, this book offers readers a logical extension to the story of Operation Medusa, in particular showing how Taliban strategy and tactics adapted quickly after the blow they had been dealt.

B. BOOKS ABOUT SOLDIERING I TURNED TO WHEN DECIDING HOW TO FIGHT THE TALIBAN

A Soldier's Story
BY OMAR N. BRADLEY
An outstanding account of Bradley's time with Patton. The movie *Patton* was based on this book. I like that this work understates Bradley as a leader, which is endearing to me. This is what a leader is supposed to be like.

Stalingrad: The Fateful Siege: 1942–1943
BY ANTONY BEEVOR
Antony Beevor is perhaps the best storyteller in the canon of military history. His ability to grip the reader is remarkable. The story about Stalingrad is one of determination and the enormous cost of achieving a mission that was critical to the overall campaign. It was a victory and

defeat that affected both sides accordingly. These lessons would influence the outcome of our fight in Medusa.

Dereliction of Duty: Johnson, McNamara, the Joint Chiefs of Staff, & the Lies That Led to Vietnam
BY H.R. MCMASTER

An outstanding book about the situation at the time and the failure of the system. Cutting stuff. Failing to speak truth to power can lead to devastating results. I surrounded myself with a team who understood the need to tell me what I needed to hear, not what I wanted to hear. As this book shows, the consequences of playing up to the boss are both time-defeating and potentially strategically and tactically disastrous.

Hell in a Very Small Place: The Siege of Dien Bien Phu
BY BERNARD FALL

Fall is perhaps the best of all writers who have tackled the war in Indochina. His book is a personal favourite, in part because of its gripping retelling of the siege of Dien Bien Phu.

Defeat into Victory
BY FIELD MARSHAL VISCOUNT WILLIAM SLIM

A tremendous account of what Slim went through in the 1940s building his army and fighting the Japanese, and in many ways an analogy for the story of the southern coalition in Afghanistan fighting the Taliban.

Monty: The Making of a General: 1887–1942
BY NIGEL HAMILTON

This is the book I thought of when OEF commander Karl Eikenberry first grilled me on what our Canadian task force could possibly contribute to the fight in Afghanistan. It's the outstanding biography of Field Marshal Viscount Montgomery, revealing his strategies, complex relationships with military leaders, and fascinating details about his life as a soldier.

CREDIT OUR PHOTOGRAPHERS

Whenever the Canadian military moves into action abroad, photographers and videographers go with them as often as possible to document unfolding events. These specially trained professionals are themselves members of the Canadian Armed Forces. They live among their comrades and share in their adventures through both calm and combat. Each scene they capture tells a unique story, and over time their images form a collection that speaks volumes about the nature of missions such as those we undertook in Afghanistan. Housed within the Department of National Defence, the archive of their work is a rich resource for all students of history. And in books such as this one, even a small collection functions as a narrative all its own. As we researched this book, our longstanding appreciation for these photographers was deepened yet again. While the credit they receive here is just the simple phrase DND Combat Camera, we proudly salute these men and women for their sense of duty, strength of character, and mastery of art.

COVER	Gregory Moon		PAGE 26	DND Combat Camera
PAGE 4	DND Combat Camera		PAGE 29	DND Combat Camera
PAGE 5	DND Combat Camera		PAGE 35	DND Combat Camera
PAGE 8	DND Combat Camera		PAGE 41	DND Combat Camera
PAGE 18	DND Combat Camera		PAGE 43	Christian Buchan

PAGE 56	DND Combat Camera	PAGE 136	DND Combat Camera
PAGE 57	DND Combat Camera	PAGE 139	Courtesy of the US Army
PAGE 62	DND Combat Camera	PAGE 142	DND Combat Camera
PAGE 65	Musadeq Sadeq/AP/Press	PAGE 148	DND Combat Camera
PAGE 69	Stiff (Ottawa)	PAGE 149	DND Combat Camera
PAGE 77	DND Combat Camera	PAGE 154	DND Combat Camera
PAGE 92	Mike Wright	PAGE 156	DND Combat Camera
PAGE 93	David Fraser	PAGE 177	DND Combat Camera
PAGE 104	Mike Wright	PAGE 184	DND Combat Camera
PAGE 105	DND Combat Camera	PAGE 186	DND Combat Camera
PAGE 111	Mike Wright	PAGE 189	DND Combat Camera
PAGE 118	DND Combat Camera	PAGE 192	DND Combat Camera
PAGE 123	DND Combat Camera	PAGE 194	DND Combat Camera
PAGE 126	DND Combat Camera	PAGE 207	Adam Seegmiller
PAGE 127	Shane Schreiber	PAGE 210	DND Combat Camera
PAGE 131	William Irving	PAGE 211	David Fraser
PAGE 133	DND Combat Camera	PAGE 214	Adam Seegmiller

AUTHOR PHOTOS
PAGE 246   Mike MacDonald
PAGE 247   Vadim Daniel

ENDPAPERS Stiff (Ottawa)

DECIPHER OUR ACRONYMS

1 RCR	1st Battalion, The Royal Canadian Regiment
2-4	2nd Battalion, 4th Infantry Regiment (United States)
2-87	2nd Battalion, 87th Infantry Regiment (United States)
2IC	second-in-command
3 PARA	3rd Battalion, Parachute Regiment
AB	able seaman
ADZ	Afghan Development Zone
AFF	Afghan Freedom Fighters
AH	attack helicopter
AMA	artillery manoeuvre area
ANDS	Afghanistan National Development Strategy
ARRC	Allied Rapid Reaction Corps (NATO)
CAF	Canadian Armed Forces
CAS	combat air support or close air support
CCP	casualty collection point
CEFCOM	Canadian Expeditionary Force Command
CER	Combat Engineer Regiment
CHOPS	chief of operations
CIDA	Canadian International Development Agency
CIMIC	civilian military cooperation
CJTF-76	Combined Joint Task Force 76

COMISAF	Commander International Security Assistance Force
CONOP	concept of operations
COY	company
CPL	corporal
CPO	chief petty officer
CQ	company quartermaster
CSM	company sergeant major
CTF	combined task force
CWO	chief warrant officer
DFAIT	Department of Foreign Affairs and International Trade
EOD	explosive ordnance disposal
F2T2EA	Find, Fix, Track, Target, Engage & Assess
F3EA	Find, Fix, Finish, Exploit & Analyze
FAC	forward air controller
FDU	fleet diving unit
FOB	forward operating base
FOM	freedom of movement
FOO	forward observation officer
FSM	formation sergeant major
GOA	Government of Afghanistan
G-WAGEN	Geländewagen, a cross-country vehicle
HQ	headquarters
HUMINT	human intelligence
IAW	in accordance with
IED	improvised explosive device
IOT	in order to
ISAF	International Security Assistance Force
ISTAR	intelligence, surveillance, target acquisition and reconnaissance
IVO	in the vicinity of
JSOTF	Joint Special Operations Task Force
JSTARS	joint surveillance target attack radar system
JTF 2	Joint Task Force 2
KAF	Kandahar Airfield

KIA	killed in action
KLE	key leader engagement
LAV	light armoured vehicle
LCDR	lieutenant commander
LGEN	lieutenant general
LN	local nationals
LT	lieutenant
MAJ	major
MEDEVAC	medical evacuation
MEWT	mobile electronic warfare team
MGEN	major general
MS	master seaman
MWO	master warrant officer
NAI	named area of interest
NATO	North Atlantic Treaty Organization
NCE	national contingent element
NCO	non-commissioned officer
NDHQ	National Defence Headquarters (Canada)
NDS	National Directorate of Security (Afghanistan)
NORAD	North American Aerospace Defense Command
NORTHCOM	United States Northern Command
ODA	Operational Detachment Alpha
ODB	Operational Detachment Bravo
OEF	Operation Enduring Freedom
OS	ordinary seaman
PAO	public affairs officer
PED	processing, exploitation and dissemination
PO	petty officer
PPCLI	Princess Patricia's Canadian Light Infantry
PRT	provincial reconstruction team
PSYOPS	psychological operations
PTE	private
RC EAST	Regional Command East

244 | OPERATION MEDUSA

RCMI	Royal Canadian Military Institute
RCR	The Royal Canadian Regiment
RC SOUTH	Regional Command South
RIP	relief in place
RPG	rocket-propelled grenade
RSM	regimental sergeant major
RTE	route
SA	situational awareness
SACEUR	Supreme Allied Commander Europe
SIED	suicide improvised explosive device
SIGACTS	significant activities
SIGINT	signals intelligence
SGT	sergeant
SLT	sub-lieutenant
SOF	special operations forces
TAC	tactical team
TB	Taliban
TCCC	tactical combat casualty care
TF	task force
TIC	troops in contact
TOC	tactical operations centre
TOCA	transfer of command authority
TTP	tactics, techniques and procedures
TUAV	tactical unmanned aerial vehicle
VSA	vital signs absent
UAV	unmanned aerial vehicle
UN	United Nations
USAID	United States Agency for International Development
WO	warrant officer

ACKNOWLEDGEMENTS

Events endured in the heat of battle are not always retrieved easily or accurately in the peace that follows. I am grateful to many people who took the time to consult their colleagues, correspondence and diaries to help us clarify what happened when. In particular, we salute David "Buck" Buchanan, Ben Freakley, Mike Gauthier, Bill "Mother" Irving, Allan "Dooner" Muldoon, David Richards, Shane Schreiber, Adam "Seegy" Seegmiller and Mike Wright for helping us make sure that what we have said is true. A quiet nod of thanks to Greg "Mooner" Moon who allowed us to use his haunting photograph of four members of the Posse for our cover.

I thank the talented staff of Stiff in Ottawa for their research, design and the dogged transcription of many dozens of interviews thick with acronyms and foreign place names. James Hanington, Kelsey Hooper, Anna Jackson, Deborah Johnson, Donna Johnson, Sarah MacDonell, Alex Marinelli, Christena Morrell, Lee Pakkala and Glenna Tapper all have our deep gratitude. For thoughtful guidance on the shape and tone of the overall manuscript I thank Jane Burnell. Jane spent many dozens of hours reading successive drafts and graciously endured my constant badgering. For early help in the development of the charts in this book I salute Chester "Terry" Warner of the Canadian Armed Forces Mapping and Charting Establishment, Derek Sarty of Gaynor Sarty in Halifax, Kelly MacKinnon in Kingston, and the staff of World of Maps in Ottawa. Extra notes of thanks go to Lee Pakkala at Stiff who designed the charts appearing on the endpapers inside our front and back covers, and to Christena Morrell at Stiff who ably supported our research in the busy final stages. As my mentor throughout the rotation, Andy Leslie was a true battle buddy whose wise counsel helped make sense of seemingly unmanageable events before, during and following the events described in this book.

I want to thank my co-author Brian Hanington for his patience and good humour listening to hours, days, weeks and months of interviews, explanations of doctrine, and the exciting, the boring and the minutiae of what made up Operation Medusa. Brian has gone from being a well-read civilian to being an honorary member of the Posse. Brian now knows as much as each of us, and his ability to take our thoughts and turn them into words has made the writing of this book possible. He has been a good book fire-team partner. I will always be very appreciative of his efforts. Brian and I owe much to Tom Jenkins, who had the happy thought of suggesting we work together; this volume is but the first result of the partnership trio that Tom made possible. Brian and I had unwavering support throughout from our publishers at McClelland & Stewart, particularly from the quintet of experts who brought this project into being: our colleague and friend Doug Pepper gave us every assistance and encouragement; Kimberlee Hesas managed a complex project within a wildly compressed timeframe; Gemma Wain offered meticulous editorial criticism and guidance that allowed us to improve countless passages in our text; Scott Richardson designed the book with his trademark passion and ingenuity; and Erin Cooper implemented that design in a layout that is elegant and simple.

Above all else, I wish to thank the families who supported all of us over there. In particular, I salute the Fraser family for whom our ordeal in Afghanistan was distressing and in ways destructive. Thank you Poppie, Andrew, Daniel, Marjorie, Ian, and Barb and Regis Gagne. Without the support of our families, none of us could have focused on what was ahead of us, and the constant danger would have been far more difficult to bear. Words will never describe our collective appreciation. I dedicate this book to them.

MAJOR GENERAL (RET'D) DAVID FRASER, CMM, MSC, MSM, CD

David Fraser is a major general of the Canadian Armed Forces. He was the commander of the multinational brigade for Regional Command South in Afghanistan's southern provinces in 2006. One of the most decorated generals in CAF history, Fraser was the commander of Operation Medusa in Afghanistan, the largest combat engagement of Canadian armed forces in over fifty years. Upon leaving the CAF, David joined the private sector and, with his partners, created Blue Goose Pure Foods. Since then, he has taken his leadership and business skills to other companies, including INKAS Armored Vehicle Manufacturing where he served as chief operations officer. Today, David works with BMO Financial Group on its Canadian Defence Community Banking program. His honours and awards include Commander of Military Merit, Canadian Meritorious Service Cross, Meritorious Service Medal, United States Legion of Honor and Bronze Star (for service in Afghanistan), and awards from the Netherlands, Poland and NATO. He is the recipient of the Vimy Award for outstanding contributions towards the security and defence of Canada and the preservation of our democratic values, and the Atlantic Council Award for International Leadership. David Fraser lives in Toronto, Canada.

BRIAN HANINGTON

Son of a Canadian admiral and a CBC television talk-show host, Brian
Hanington fell comfortably into a life related to military journalism.
Following a decade as a naval rating and then officer in both seagoing
and public information roles, he focused on writing. He became pub-
lisher and editor of the *Maritime Command Trident*, a biweekly newspaper
for the military community; wrote and published *Every Popish Person*, a
bestselling history of Nova Scotia extensively profiling the military presence in Halifax, and served as a speechwriter to the Minister of National
Defence. He has since written or edited more than a dozen books, lectured
in over twenty countries, and crafted speeches and correspondence for
prime ministers, cabinet ministers, bishops, admirals, generals, film stars,
knights, and His Holiness John Paul II. He is currently chairman of Stiff,
the Ottawa-based communications agency he founded in 1988.

A NOTE ABOUT THE TYPE

Operation Medusa is set in Electra, designed in 1935 by William Addison Dwiggins. A popular face for book-length work since its release, Electra is noted for its evenness and high legibility in both text sizes and display settings.

OPERATION MEDUSA: THE BATTLE

21°E   24°E   27°E

1 AUG 19-SEP 2, 2006 PAGES 134-143
Operation Medusa commences with key-leader engagement and bombardment of Taliban targets.

2 AUG 30, 2006 PAGE 169
Taliban attacks Task Force 31 near Red Desert.

3 SEP 2, 2006 PAGE 150
RAF Nimrod crashes south of Kandahar Airfield.

4 SEP 3, 2006 PAGE 151
Charles Company crosses Arghandab River to establish beachhead.

5 SEP 3, 2006 PAGE 152
Charles Company ambushed. Withdraws back across river.

6 SEP 4, 2006 PAGE 165
Charles Company strafed by USAF Warthog A10.

7 SEP 2-7, 2006 PAGES 169-180
Task Force 31 takes Sperwan Ghar and clears Objective Billiards.

8 SEP 9, 2006 PAGE 182
Task Force Grizzly and ISTAR Squadron cover 1RCR deployment north to PB Wilson.

9 SEP 9, 2006 PAGE 190
Task Force 31 takes Siah Choy and clears Objective Tennis.

10 SEP 10-12, 2006 PAGE 168
A & Bravo Companies & TF Mohawk clear Objectives Cricket & Lacrosse.

11 SEP 14, 2006 PAGE 190
Task Force Grizzly crosses river to help clear Objective Rugby.

12 SEP 15, 2006 PAGE 191
Canadians retake white schoolhouse and clear Objective Rugby.

13 SEP 16, 2006 PAGE 191
Coalition forces clear Objective Baseball. Taliban pushed past 24 Easting.

14 SEP 17, 2006 PAGE 191
Operation Medusa declared concluded.

CARTOGRAPHY BY STIFF (OTTAWA)

HIGHWAY 1 (S

13

OBJECTIVE:
BASEBALL

P A N

SIAH CHOY

OBJECTIVE:
TENNIS **9**

ARGHANDAB RIVER

ZANGABAD GHAR

2